TABLE OF CONTENTS

Practice Test #1

1. Which of the following best describes how Fauvism artists departed from previous styles?

a. They used small dots of pure color to let the eye blend the colors together, rather than mixing colors on the palette.
b. They used intense, unnatural colors and disregarded proportions rather than using realistic colors and portraying proportions accurately.
c. They portrayed nonrepresentational subjects rather than portraying recognizable subjects in their artwork.
d. They reduced subjects into geometric shapes and primary colors rather than faithfully representing recognizable subjects.

2. Which of the following best describes form, which is an element of art?

a. The positive and negative areas of an artwork
b. A flat element with height and width
c. The way things feel or look like they may feel in an artwork
d. A three-dimensional shape that has width, depth, and height

3. Which of the following types of architectural vaults is shown in this image?

a. Groin vault
b. Barrel vault
c. Rib vault
d. Tunnel vault

4. Which of the following artists did NOT paint in the color field style?

a. Vladimir Tatlin
b. Mark Rothko
c. Clyfford Still
d. Frank Stella

5. Which of the following is NOT a function of linseed oil when used for oil painting?

a. Helps to maintain the flexibility of oil paint
b. Makes the oil paint more fluid and transparent
c. Cleans and conditions paintbrushes
d. Increases the drying time of oil paint

6. Which of the following best describes willow charcoal?

a. Graphite shaped into thin sticks
b. Pigment bound with gum arabic
c. Organic materials bound with a wax binder
d. Sticks burnt in a kiln without air

7. Of these architectural designs, which best embodies the theory of "form follows function"?

a. An office building is designed inside a repurposed department store.
b. A bank is designed with a facade to resemble a Greek temple.
c. A stadium is designed to have room for spectators surrounding a central field for the players.
d. A college campus is designed with walking paths that form intricate geometric designs.

8. Which of the following most accurately describes the art technique of pouncing?

a. A decorative method of writing that involves a broad-tipped pen
b. A method similar to tracing that involves pricking holes in paper and forcing a powder through those holes
c. A method of sketching that involves large, broad gestures with the arm and hand to capture the subject
d. A method of drawing that involves creating lines perpendicular to each other to create values

9. Which of the following does NOT describe an advantage of creating an artwork on a toned paper or canvas, instead of the usual white ground?

a. A dark-toned ground can serve as the darker tones in the artwork.
b. A toned ground can be less intimidating to begin working on than a white ground.
c. A toned ground will often be less expensive than a white ground for artwork.
d. A medium-toned ground can allow the artist to build up both highlights and shadows in the artwork.

10. Which of the following architectural styles is characterized by decorative timbering and a steeply pitched roof, as shown in this image?

a. Tudor
b. Queen Anne
c. Art Deco
d. Italianate

11. Which of the following best describes the aquatint printmaking process?

a. Melting fine particles of acid-resistant material onto a metal plate, then etching the plate with acid
b. Alternately scraping smooth and roughening a metal plate to create light areas and shading
c. Carving a block with a gouge, leaving the raised parts of the block as the positive image
d. Arranging materials onto a surface to create a raised textured print

12. Which of the following terms best describes the contrast between a dark-skinned figure wearing dark clothes sitting next to a pale-skinned figure wearing white clothing?

a. Transformation
b. Contextualization
c. Appropriation
d. Juxtaposition

13. Which of the following best describes the motivations of the Expressionist artists?

a. To minimize their concepts into simple geometric forms
b. To present their ideas subjectively and express emotions through their artwork
c. To capture the effects of light on their subjects through color
d. To elevate popular culture in artwork and challenge the traditions of art

14. Which of the following themes did Keith Haring often address in his murals and artwork?

a. Global warming and environmental issues
b. Immigration and social justice
c. Acquired immunodeficiency syndrome (AIDS) and homosexuality
d. Industry and progress

15. Which of the following metals is usually added to silver to create sterling silver?

a. Copper
b. Bronze
c. Gold
d. Pewter

16. This painting shows a strong contrast between the dark background and the highlights on the subject. Which of the following is this technique an example of?

a. Chiaroscuro
b. Sfumato
c. Fresco
d. Intonaco

17. Which of the following color combinations could be used to create an analogous color scheme?

a. Red, yellow, and blue
b. Red, orange, green, and blue
c. Yellow, red-violet, and blue-violet
d. Green, blue-green, and blue

18. Which of the following describes how a student could use their metacognitive skills in the art classroom?

a. Answering selected response questions about a period of art history
b. Tracing a drawing made by a famous artist
c. Creating an artwork with two different materials
d. Making revisions on their sketches after revisiting their goals for an artwork

19. Which of the following was NOT an innovation contributed to the art world during the Renaissance period?

a. Linear perspective
b. Egg tempera
c. Foreshortening
d. Sfumato

20. An artist wishes to mask off an area of an artwork to prevent paint from changing that area. Which of the following materials would they use?

a. Tissue paper
b. Rice paper
c. Frisket
d. Linseed oil

21. Which of the following best describes what a camera's ISO setting adjusts?

a. The size of the lens opening
b. The image sensor's sensitivity to light
c. The depth of field
d. The shutter speed

22. An artist wants to use an oil- or wax-based media and a water-based media in one project. Which of the following describes the best way to layer these media?

a. Oil paint layered on top of acrylic paint
b. Gouache layered on top of oil pastels
c. Watercolor layered on top of encaustic
d. Tempera layered on top of crayon

23. Which of the following best describes the work of Romare Bearden?

a. Detailed collages of African-American life
b. Life-sized silhouettes of slave scenes
c. Miniature sculptures encouraging social justice
d. Street art highlighting the plight of poor neighborhoods

24. Which of the following pigments is NOT considered hazardous due to its use of toxic metals?

a. Cadmium red
b. Chrome yellow
c. Yellow ochre
d. Cobalt blue

25. Which of the following best describes the difference between watercolor paint and gouache paint?

a. Gouache is used in a thick impasto technique, whereas watercolor is painted in thin layers.
b. Gouache is available only in neutral tones, whereas watercolor is available in a full range of colors.
c. Gouache is used for illustration work, whereas watercolor is used for fine art.
d. Gouache is opaque, whereas watercolor is transparent.

26. This woman is using a wax-resist dyeing method to decorate fabric. Which of the following is the correct term for this technique?

a. Intaglio
b. Batik
c. Etching
d. Inlay

27. Artists Eugène Delacroix, Théodore Géricault, and Thomas Cole are all associated with which of the following art movements?

a. Romanticism
b. Surrealism
c. Art Nouveau
d. Neoclassicism

28. This painting gives the illusion of viewing space from below on a ceiling, using foreshortened figures. Which of the following is the correct term for this technique?

a. Chiaroscuro
b. Di sotto in su
c. Fresco
d. Pentimento

29. Of these architectural designs, which best describes an Art Nouveau-style building?

a. A symmetrical design with a pediment and Corinthian columns
b. An open floor plan with a low-pitched roof, strings of windows, and long horizontal lines
c. A rectangular, utilitarian plan with solid walls and without ornamentation
d. An asymmetrical facade with decorations including butterflies, orchids, and water lilies

30. In this still life, which technique does the artist use to create visual interest?

a. The arrangement in the artwork forms a pattern.
b. The still life is comprised of an analogous color scheme.
c. A variety of shapes are arranged throughout the work.
d. The objects in the still life are arranged asymmetrically.

31. Which of the following is NOT an advantage of using acrylic paint instead of oil paint?

a. Acrylic paint can be cleaned up with soap and water, instead of needing solvents for cleaning.
b. Acrylic paint can be thinned with water, whereas oil paints require oils and solvents.
c. Acrylic paints are all nontoxic, unlike oil paints.
d. Acrylic paints dry much more quickly than oil paints, allowing artists to produce work more quickly.

32. A watercolor artist wishes to stretch his watercolor paper prior to starting a painting. Which of the following best describes a proper method to stretch the paper?

a. The paper is soaked with water and then manually stretched by hand in all directions.
b. The paper is soaked with water, placed on a board, then taped around the edges with gummed paper tape and allowed to dry overnight.
c. The paper is soaked with water, hung with clips from a rail, and weights are hung off the bottom of the paper.
d. The paper is soaked with water and then rolled with a wooden pin to remove the excess water.

33. An artist needs to be able to erase various parts of a drawing without leaving pieces of eraser on the paper and without harming the surface. Which type of eraser would work best for this purpose?

a. Kneaded eraser
b. Art gum eraser
c. Pink pearl eraser
d. Vinyl eraser

34. Which of the following best describes the purpose of artwork in Ancient Egypt?

a. It was mostly created for tombs and for the afterlife.
b. Artwork was created to decorate the pyramids.
c. It was mainly jewelry to be worn by the rulers of Egypt.
d. Artwork was mostly in the form of paintings to decorate the walls of palaces.

35. Which of the following is correct in regard to following an ethical standard related to creating artwork?

a. Using public domain images without checking the fine print for restrictions
b. Avoiding copyright issues by working from life or using your own photographs
c. Copying a famous artwork and publishing it as your own work
d. Using another artist's ideas without asking for permission beforehand

36. Which of the following regions would this sculpture have likely originated from?

a. Europe
b. Asia
c. Africa
d. North America

37. Which of the following best describes the stage of clay called slip?

a. Clay that is partially dry but not yet completely dry
b. Clay that is completely dry but has not been fired yet
c. Clay that has been fired once in a kiln
d. A mix of clay and water with a runny consistency

38. Which of the following best describes the significance of the Armory Show in 1913?

a. It was the first exhibition to showcase Realist artists in Europe.
b. It was the first art show that showcased mainly Minimalist artists.
c. It was the first art show to take place in a major military location.
d. It was the first major modern art exhibition in America.

39. Which of the following types of perspective is shown in this image?

a. One-point perspective
b. Two-point perspective
c. Three-point perspective
d. Four-point perspective

40. Which of the following best describes the nave of a church?

a. A center aisle
b. A vaulted, semicircular structure at the end of the aisle
c. A circular opening in the center of a dome
d. A flat, upright column inset in a wall

41. Which of the following best describes the process of enameling?

a. Two metals are joined together to create a stronger type of metal.
b. Sheets of glass are melted with metal leading in between.
c. Liquid glaze is fired onto a ceramic piece, which then forms into a shiny glaze.
d. Powdered glass is fused to a surface and melted to a smooth, shiny coating.

42. Which of the following metalworking techniques is shown in this image?

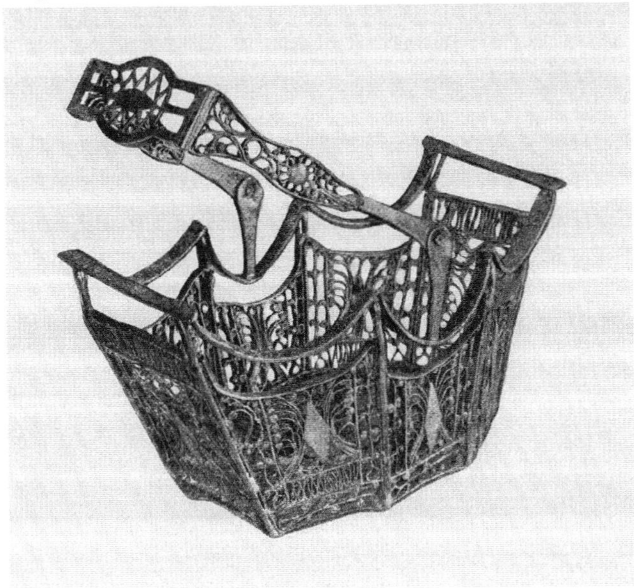

a. Etching
b. Lost wax casting
c. Stamping
d. Filigree

43. On a camera, what is the name of this part where the flash would attach to?

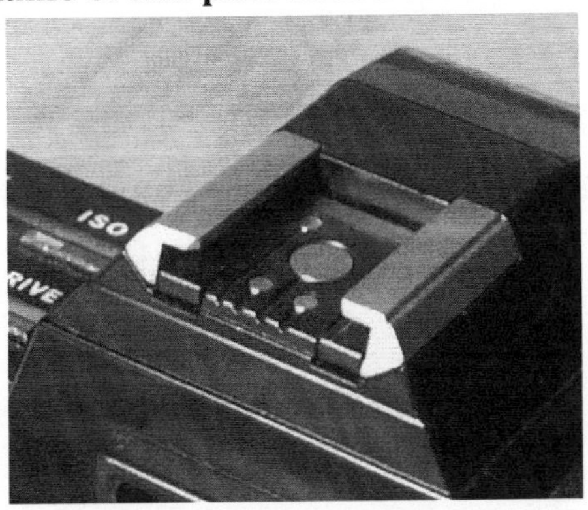

a. F-stop
b. Hot shoe
c. Shutter release
d. Emulsion plate

44. Which of the following best describes context as related to artwork?

a. The physical materials used by an artist to create an artwork
b. The elements or principles used within a work
c. The conditions or circumstances around which something is made
d. The ways in which an artist uses their skills to create a work

45. Which of the following genres of photography was generally NOT accepted as fine art prior to the 1970s?

a. Nudes
b. Fashion
c. Portraits
d. Landscapes

46. Which of the following best describes the mass tone of a paint pigment?

a. The color of a paint straight from the tube
b. The name of the color of the paint
c. The opacity of the pigment
d. How permanent the pigment is

47. Which of the following issues could occur if an oil painting is varnished too early?

a. The varnish could peel off of the painting.
b. The varnish could be too easily removable.
c. The varnish could bring a more even sheen to the surface.
d. The varnish could turn tacky and not dry.

48. Which of the following was NOT a role of an apprentice to a master artist during the Renaissance?

a. Communicating with patrons
b. Cleaning paintbrushes
c. Grinding pigments
d. Preparing surfaces for paintings

49. In intaglio printmaking, ink is squeegeed across the plate, forcing the ink into the lines. Which of the following steps would come next in this process?

a. A dampened sheet of etching paper is laid on top of the plate.
b. Felt blankets are placed on top of the paper.
c. The plate is then wiped with a rag.
d. The plate is rolled between two steel rollers on an etching press.

50. The artists Willem de Kooning, Jackson Pollock, and Franz Kline are all associated with which art movement?

a. De Stijl
b. Abstract Expressionism
c. Dada
d. Minimalism

51. Which of the following would be the correct method of creating a tint of the color red?

a. Adding black to red
b. Adding white to red
c. Adding blue to red
d. Adding yellow to red

52. The line in this artwork where the sky meets the ground is called which of the following?

a. The proportional line
b. The perspective line
c. The axis line
d. The horizon line

53. Which of the following describes a bas relief sculpture?

a. A sculpture created in the round to be viewed from all angles
b. A sculpture created around a framework or armature
c. A sculpture attached to a back slab and projecting slightly
d. A sculpture attached to a back slab and projecting significantly

54. Which of the following is the name given to the small Paleolithic sculptures shaped like women with enlarged stomachs and breasts that were likely used as fertility symbols?

a. Junos
b. Jupiters
c. Venuses
d. Mercuries

55. Which of the following is the correct name for this decorated semicircular alcove in a wall of a mosque, indicating the point nearest to Mecca?

a. Mihrab
b. Arabesque
c. Madrasa
d. Minbar

56. Which of the following best describes a motivation behind the iconoclasm in the Byzantine Empire in the 700s?

a. Christian images were seen as idols, which opposed the Old Testament prohibition of idolatry.
b. Artists began to purposely depict Christianity incorrectly, so the artwork was prohibited.
c. Artwork depicting Christianity had been a focus for so long that it was time to focus artwork on new subjects.
d. In light of debates of whether artwork was correctly depicting scenes from Christianity, these scenes were subsequently banned.

57. Which of the following best describes proportion in an artwork?

a. A way that forms are organized in space
b. A line along which forms are organized
c. The relationships of sizes of various elements within the artwork
d. The shape of the subject in an artwork

58. Which of the following accurately describes a difference between alkyd paints and traditional oil paints?

a. Alkyds blend more easily than oils.
b. Alkyds are thicker than oils.
c. Alkyds dry glossier than oils.
d. Alkyds dry more quickly than oils.

59. Which of the following best describes the difference between a gargoyle and a grotesque?

a. A gargoyle depicts a creature with wings, whereas a grotesque depicts a person.
b. A gargoyle is situated at the top of a building, whereas a grotesque can decorate any part of a building.
c. A gargoyle is only on the corner of buildings, whereas a grotesque can line any wall of a building.
d. A gargoyle has a waterspout, whereas a grotesque does not.

60. In this image, the figure has a dynamic pose, with the weight on one leg and the shoulders at an opposite angle from the hips. This pose is called which one of the following?

a. Sprezzatura
b. Pentimento
c. Chiaroscuro
d. Contrapposto

61. Which of the following was NOT a commonality among the artists of the New York School in the 1940s?

a. They agreed on styles and theories of art.
b. They were nearly all in their twenties and thirties.
c. Many of them had worked on the WPA.
d. They all believed in the individuality of the artist.

62. Which of the following describes how Frank Stella purposely removed expressive content from his artwork?

a. He used straight edges rather than any curved forms.
b. He eliminated visible brushstrokes, gesture, and definition of the surface.
c. He only used one color at a time on each painting.
d. He worked only in grayscale, without using any other colors in his artwork.

63. If an artist wishes to use an opaque paint to create an illustration with a matte sheen that could be reworked with water if needed, which of the following paints would be most appropriate to use?

a. Acrylic
b. Watercolor
c. Oil
d. Gouache

64. Which of the following cultures would include this figure as a sculptural form?

a. China
b. Egypt
c. India
d. Mongolia

65. Which of the following best describes the photography process of exposure bracketing?

a. Setting the exposure for your photograph prior to taking the photo
b. The process of deciding on the exposure for your photograph using a device to measure the light
c. Taking one photograph at the correct exposure, one overexposed, and one underexposed
d. Programming a digital camera to take the photograph using the proper exposure

66. Which of the following graphic file formats should be used if you need a web graphic with transparency?

a. .jpg
b. .gif
c. .tif
d. .raw

67. Which of the following would a hake brush be best suited for when painting?

a. Laying large, flat areas of color in a watercolor painting
b. Adding small areas of detail in an oil painting
c. Painting repeated layers of egg tempera
d. Creating an acrylic painting from start to finish

68. Which of the following English artists was NOT credited with establishing watercolor as an independent painting medium?

a. Thomas Girtin
b. Paul Sandby
c. Joseph Mallord William Turner
d. William H. Bartlett

69. Which of the following is a stipulation of the cultural heritage sites that UNESCO protects and preserves?

a. They must be man-made.
b. They must be more than 1 million years old.
c. They must be made only of natural materials.
d. They must receive over 500,000 visitors a year.

70. Which of the following is the correct term for this four-sided architectural element with a pyramidal top?

a. Caryatid
b. Entablature
c. Peristyle
d. Obelisk

71. Which of the following best describes the traditional Japanese aesthetic of wabi-sabi?

a. A concentration on simple forms
b. A portrayal of transcendent landscapes
c. An acceptance of imperfections
d. A focus on curving lines rather than straight

72. An art critic analyzes an artwork based on the use of elements and principles, not delving into the context associated with the artwork. Which of the following criticism theories is this critic using?

a. Formalism
b. Expressionism
c. Deconstructivism
d. Representationalism

73. Which of the following describes the symmetry that would be found in a rose window of a Gothic-style cathedral?

a. Asymmetrical
b. Radial
c. Reflection
d. Reciprocal

74. Which of the following painters was NOT an artist in the Hudson River School?

a. Thomas Cole
b. Albert Bierstadt
c. Frederic Edwin Church
d. Hans Fredrik Gude

75. Which of the following would NOT be recommended to improve this still life?

a. Include only two of the objects shown, instead of three.
b. Flatten the table a bit so the objects do not look like they will slide off.
c. More consistently round the edges of the rounded objects.
d. Make objects that are close together either overlap more or not touch at all, rather than barely touch.

76. Which of the following elements of art did Keith Haring's artwork most focus on?

a. Color
b. Line
c. Value
d. Texture

77. Which of the following best describes the difference between the principles of design pattern and rhythm?

a. A pattern repeats elements in the same order, whereas rhythm repeats elements with variation.
b. A pattern focuses on shapes, whereas rhythm focuses on line.
c. A pattern will add elements as it progresses, whereas rhythm will repeat the same elements.
d. A pattern will repeat elements in a grid, whereas rhythm repeats elements in a line.

78. Which of the following best describes Philip Pearlstein's artistic process?

a. Applying drips and splatters of paint to a horizontal canvas
b. Copying photographs using a grid system
c. Creating photorealistic paintings from live models
d. Creating large areas of color that reach the edges of the canvas

79. Which of the following is a theme that Cindy Sherman has explored in a photographic series?

a. The homeless population in major cities
b. Deviant and marginalized people
c. The impact of businesses on the environment
d. The roles of women in society

80. If an artist is said to be a contemporary of another artist, which of the following is true?

a. The artists worked with the same materials.
b. The artists worked in the same style.
c. The artists lived at the same time.
d. The artists lived in the same country.

81. Which of the following is an example of appropriation?

a. Kara Walker's use of silhouettes in her artwork *Darkytown Rebellion*
b. The Guerrilla Girls' use of the *Grande Odalisque* in *Do Women Have to Be Naked to Get into the Met. Museum?*
c. David Smith's use of stainless steel in *Cubi XII*
d. Alexander Calder's use of moving parts in his mobile sculptures

82. Which of the following types of domes are shown in this image?

a. Onion domes
b. Geodesic domes
c. Monolithic domes
d. Beehive domes

83. Which of the following best describes the goal of Surrealist art?

a. To bypass reason and unlock ideas from the unconscious mind
b. To capture the effect of lighting on a scene
c. To simultaneously show interlocking planes used to construct a scene
d. To react against the bourgeois and depart from traditional values of art

84. Which of the following best describes fine art versus applied art?

a. Fine art includes paintings and drawings, whereas applied art includes all forms of sculpture.
b. Fine art includes any art shown in museums, whereas applied art occurs in educational contexts.
c. Fine art refers to artwork that was produced before the contemporary period, and applied art is art produced in or after the contemporary period.
d. Fine art has no functional purpose other than being aesthetically, artistically, or intellectually pleasing or stimulating, whereas applied art serves a purpose.

85. Which of the following would have been created with a subtractive sculpture technique?

a. Robert Rauschenberg's *Bed*
b. Claes Oldenburg and Coosje van Bruggen's *Spoonbridge and Cherry*
c. Jeff Koons' *Balloon Dog*
d. Michelangelo's *David*

86. Which of the following types of paints would have been used on this illuminated manuscript from the Middle Ages?

a. Gouache
b. Acrylic
c. Tempera
d. Oil

87. Which of the following best describes the drawing tool called a tortillon?

a. A thicker type of drawing paper that is available in hot-pressed or cold-pressed form
b. A tightly rolled piece of paper, tapered at one end, used for blending
c. A pouch of powdered gum eraser in a mesh fabric bag
d. A flat metal sheet with various shapes cut into it for erasing

88. Which of the following types of paints replaced egg tempera in popularity in the 1500s?

a. Oil
b. Watercolor
c. Acrylic
d. Gouache

89. Which of the following is NOT an accurate safety recommendation when working with a ceramics kiln?

a. Remove all combustible materials from the kiln area.
b. Unload the kiln as soon as it is turned off.
c. Always unplug the kiln before working on electrical components.
d. Use protective glasses when looking into the kiln for long periods of time.

90. Which of the following is the correct description of repoussé metalwork?

a. Reshaping metal by removing parts to alter its shape
b. Molten metal being poured into a die and then allowed to cool
c. Metal wires that are bent to form intricate lacework designs
d. Hammering a design into metal on the reverse side to produce a low relief

91. This type of depiction of the Virgin Mary holding the dead body of Christ is called which of the following terms?

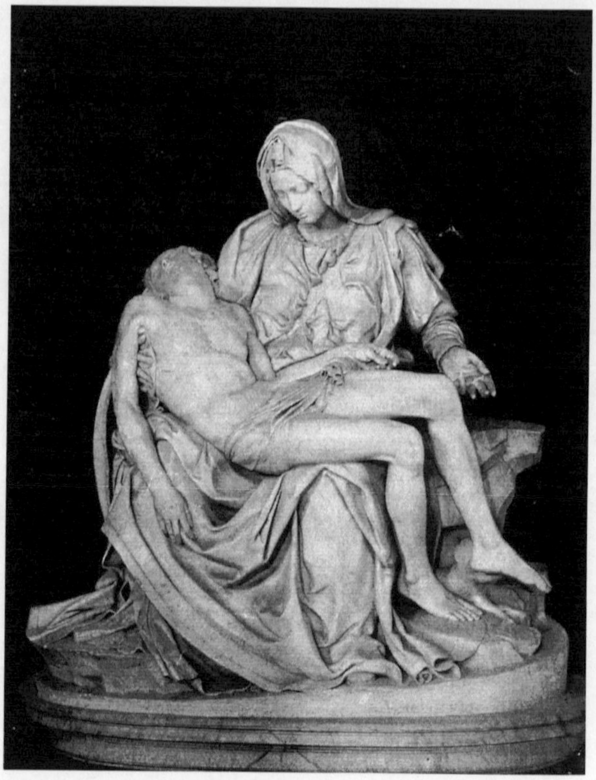

a. Pietà
b. Predella
c. Cassone
d. Campanile

92. Which of the following is the correct term for the natural color of an object when it isn't affected by lighting or other factors?

a. Absolute color
b. Actual color
c. Local color
d. Real color

93. Which of the following would be considered a figurative artwork?

a. *Broadway Boogie-Woogie* by Piet Mondrian
b. *Green and Maroon* by Mark Rothko
c. *Oath of the Horatii* by Jacques-Louis David
d. *On White II* by Wassily Kandinsky

94. Which of the following best describes the concept of repoussoir in a two-dimensional artwork?

a. Disturbing images created by juxtaposing the supernatural in a mundane setting
b. Creating tonal effects by grouping closely placed parallel lines
c. Using shading and perspective to create the illusion that the subject is three-dimensional and deceiving the eye
d. An object in the side foreground that frames the edge and directs the viewer's eye into the composition

95. Which of the following is the correct term for this mark used in graphic arts?

a. Alignment mark
b. Registration mark
c. Calibration mark
d. Positioning mark

96. Which of the following art movements relied heavily on optical color mixing?

a. Pointillism
b. Fauvism
c. Dada
d. Postmodernism

97. Which of the following is another word for a substance added to oils or varnishes to make them dry more quickly?

a. Sinopia
b. Retardataire
c. Siccative
d. Trucage

98. Which of the following best describes the printmaking technique of cerography?

a. A raised surface, sometimes linoleum or wood, is used to create the print.
b. An image is engraved into a layer of wax on a metal surface.
c. An image is carved into a metal surface, and the ink is held in these lines.
d. Ink is pressed through a fine mesh screen to produce a print.

99. Which of the following best describes the ideals of the Aesthetic movement of the mid-19th century?

a. Pursuing authenticity by depicting immigrants and working-class people
b. A belief that artists would be fulfilled by producing things that would be useful
c. A desire to unearth people's desires and fears while showing intense creativity
d. Rebellion against industrialism and maintaining that art should be a part of everyday life

100. Which of the following accurately lists the four stages of art criticism?

a. Description, analysis, interpretation, and judgment
b. Analysis, investigation, understanding, and summary
c. Dissection, inquiry, perception, and resolution
d. Itemization, classification, itemization, and recommendation

Answer Key and Explanations for Test #1

1. B: Fauvism was a departure from previous movements in that artists focused on bright, unnatural colors, bold lines, and distorted figures. Previous movements wanted to portray subjects more faithfully and use more natural colors. Impressionism, for example, sought to show the fleeting effects of light on objects and scenes, but artists still used colors that more faithfully depicted the scene and used accurate proportions as well.

2. D: Form is the space that an object takes up in three dimensions and can include geometric or organic shapes. Shape is a two-dimensional area that is flat and can also include geometric or organic shapes. Space refers to the positive and negative areas in an artwork and can include the sense of depth within the piece. The way things feel in an artwork, or appear that they would feel, is texture.

3. A: This is an example of a groin vault, which is formed when two barrel vaults intersect perpendicularly. This can also be known as a cross vault or a double-barrel vault. The edges of the intersecting vaults form the groin, which can be rounded or pointed. A barrel vault, or tunnel vault, has the appearance of a tunnel with a rounded ceiling. A rib vault, or ribbed vault, is any vault supported by masonry ribs.

4. A: Clyfford Still, Mark Rothko, and Frank Stella are artists who worked in the color field movement. This movement was characterized by large abstract fields of flat color that reach the edges of the canvas, implying that they continue past the edge. Vladimir Tatlin is best known for his work in Constructivism, which emphasized the construction of art and reflecting modern industry through abstracted artwork.

5. C: Linseed oil has many uses when working with oil paint. When mixed with oil paint, it can help to maintain the flexibility of the film, it can make the paint more fluid and transparent for blending and glazing, and it can even increase the drying time of the paint. It is not, however, used to clean and condition paintbrushes. To clean oil paints out of paintbrushes, a solvent must be used, such as turpentine or mineral spirits.

6. D: Willow charcoal is a long, thin form of charcoal made by burning willow sticks in a kiln without air. Vine charcoal is similar, made by burning grape vines in a similar manner. Compressed charcoal is a combination of organic materials pressed with a gum arabic or wax binder into a hard stick. Willow and vine charcoal are used for quick sketches and are easy to blend. They are also easy to lift, meaning erasing parts with a kneaded eraser.

7. C: The architectural term "form follows function" suggests that a building's design, or form, should be led by its function. If architecture is designed with its facade or looks primarily in mind, or if a new space is fit into a preexisting building, it does not follow this principle. When a stadium is designed with its form following its purpose, with room for spectators surrounding the central field, the form is following the function of the design.

8. B: Pouncing is a method similar to tracing, which has been used to transfer images since Renaissance times. A thin, paper-like tissue or tracing paper is laid over the original drawing, and small holes are pricked along the lines of the drawing either manually or with a pounce wheel. The drawing is then transferred by using a powder, such as chalk or charcoal, which is pushed through the holes making a dotted outline of the drawing onto a new surface.

9. C: There are many reasons to begin with a toned ground for artwork, but cost would not be a factor. Canvas is most commonly available in white, and the artist often will tone the ground to suit their needs. Using a toned ground can be less intimidating to start working on for many artists, and it can provide a middle ground for the artist to build both light and dark tones upon. The artist can also use a dark-toned ground as the darker tones in the artwork.

10. A: The Tudor style is characterized by, among other things, half-timber framing and steep roofs. The dark half-timber framing juxtaposed against a light exterior is shown here. Other characteristics of the Tudor style of architecture include diamond-shaped window panes with lead casing (also evident here), as well as dormer windows, flagstone floors, and tall, narrow windows and doors. This style was the final phase of Medieval architecture in England during the dynasty of the House of Tudor.

11. A: An aquatint print is made by first melting fine particles of acid-resistant material onto a metal plate. The plate is then etched with acid, and the resulting print can resemble a watercolor painting. When a plate is scraped smooth for light areas and roughened for dark areas, and then printed, this is called a mezzotint. A wood or linoleum block can be carved with a gouge for a relief print. A relief print can also be created using various raised textures.

12. D: Juxtaposition is a term for placing two elements side by side to invite comparison. In this example, the figure with dark clothing and dark skin is placed next to the figure with pale skin and white clothing, inviting the viewer to recognize the differences as a key point. Either of these elements alone would not have the same effect as when they are juxtaposed. Juxtaposition does not require contrasting elements to work, but placing objects side-by-side can produce intrigue.

13. B: Artists of the Expressionist movement sought to present their ideas subjectively and express emotions through artwork. They did this by distorting subjects and exaggerating colors, such as in Edvard Munch's *The Scream.* Minimalist artists minimized their subjects into simple forms and colors. Impressionist artists sought to capture the effects of light on their subject through color. Pop artists challenged the traditions of art and sought to elevate popular culture in artwork.

14. C: Keith Haring addressed many political and social themes in his artwork, but one of the main themes that he repeatedly addressed was acquired immunodeficiency syndrome (AIDS) and homosexuality. Haring was openly gay and was diagnosed with AIDS in 1988. After this, he used his artwork to increase awareness of AIDS. He also established a foundation to provide funding to AIDS organizations, among other causes. He died in 1990 due to complications from AIDS.

15. A: Sterling silver is a combination of 92.5% silver combined with 7.5% of another metal, usually copper. A blend of two metals is called an alloy, and this is usually done to increase a metal's strength and hardness. Fine silver, which is 99.9% pure silver, is much softer than this alloy. Silver can also be mixed with other metals, such as zinc or platinum, to reduce its ability to tarnish.

16. A: Chiaroscuro emphasizes the contrast between light and dark. In this example, the artist used a dark background to contrast against the highlights on the subject. This technique was pioneered by artists such as Rembrandt, Caravaggio, and da Vinci, and it is also used to emphasize the modeling when portraying three-dimensional figures. In this example, the contrast accentuates the subject, as if a spotlight was used to dramatize the lighting.

17. D: An analogous color scheme consists of colors next to each other on the color wheel. In this example, green, blue-green, and blue could be used for an analogous color scheme. Red, yellow, and blue are the primary colors. Red, orange, green, and blue could be a tetradic color scheme, forming a rectangle on the color wheel. Yellow, red-violet, and blue-violet would be a split complementary color scheme.

18. D: Metacognition is a process of thinking about one's own thought process and analyzing one's own learning. When students revisit their sketches and align them to their goals in an artwork, they are thinking about the process of their own learning and analyzing their progress toward a goal. Another metacognitive skill would be for students to analyze their artwork after it is finished and reflect on their progress toward their end product.

19. B: The Renaissance period brought many artistic innovations, including linear perspective, foreshortening, and the sfumato technique. Egg tempera was already in use well before the Renaissance era, and it was a popular medium throughout the Middle Ages. Egg tempera reached its peak during the Renaissance period, and it fell out of favor with the growing popularity of oil paint.

20. C: Frisket is a material that prevents an area of an artwork from being altered. On a watercolor painting, a liquid frisket might be used to preserve the white of the paper so the artist can paint over it. The frisket dries like a rubber and is then rubbed off after the painting dries, exposing the paper underneath. On an airbrush painting, an artist can use a thin adhesive film to cut and adhere to the surface, masking off an area of the artwork.

21. B: The ISO (ISO stands for the International Organization of Standardization, which is the governing body that standardizes camera sensitivity ratings) setting on a camera adjusts the image sensor's sensitivity to light. A higher ISO number will increase this sensitivity. This allows photographs to be taken with less light. A lower ISO number will decrease the image sensor's sensitivity for situations with more light. A higher ISO might be desirable in an indoor setting with a fast-moving subject. A lower ISO might be desirable in an outdoor setting with plenty of natural light.

22. A: When layering oil- or wax-based media with water-based media, it is always best to layer the oil- or waxed-based media on top of a water-based medium for maximum adhesion because oil or wax will repel water. In this situation, oil paints layered on top of acrylic paint will work best. Gouache, watercolors, and tempera are all water-based media, and oil pastels, encaustic, and crayon are oil- or wax-based media.

23. A: Romare Bearden was best known for his detailed collages depicting African-American life. He used clippings from magazines and created elaborate scenes of neighborhoods and other scenes including Harlem, jazz and blues musicians, and spirituality. Although he began as a painter, he later used his collage technique to express his ideas using found materials in a method similar to patchwork quilting.

24. C: Cadmium red, chrome yellow, and cobalt blue all contain toxic metals and should be handled with care. Paints should be kept separate from food or drink, and all materials should be washed after using. These paints should be kept off of skin if possible. If using a powdered pigment, a dust mask should be used. Yellow ochre is an earth pigment that contains iron oxide, which contributes to its hue.

25. D: Gouache is similar to watercolor, but it is opaque whereas watercolor is transparent. Both are water-based media. They are each used in thin layers, painted flat on the surface, and they would not be used in an impasto technique. Gouache and watercolors are both available in a full range of colors, and they are each used for fine art, although gouache is also used for commercial illustration work due to its tendency to lay in flat areas of color.

26. B: Batik is a wax-resist method used for decorating fabric. The resist is drawn onto the fabric with a tool called a canting, or it is printed on with a stamp. The artist can then dye the cloth, and the resist will keep those parts of the fabric from being dyed as well. The resist is then removed from the fabric by scraping or boiling it off. The word batik is of Javanese origin, although the process is used in many cultures for clothing and other fabrics.

27. A: Eugène Delacroix, Théodore Géricault, and Thomas Cole are all associated with the Romanticism movement, which was a movement not only in art but also in music and literature from the late 1700s to the mid-1800s. Romanticism was characterized by an emphasis on the individual and a glorification of nature and the past. In art, Romanticism focused on nature and dramatic scenes with strong lighting, evoking feelings and emotions.

28. B: Di sotto in su is an Italian term that means "seen from below." This technique involves creating a painting on a ceiling that employs foreshortened figures and/or a vanishing point to give the correct perspective as it would be seen from below. Chiaroscuro is a technique for the arrangement of light and dark in a work. Fresco is a painting technique involving wet plaster on a wall surface. Pentimento is an image concealed in a painting by a change made by the artist.

29. D: An Art Nouveau-style building would have an asymmetrical facade with ornamentation based on plant, animal, or flower designs such as peacocks, butterflies, orchids, or water lilies. The design would have curving forms and an eclectic style. The architect might also design the entire interior of the building, including the furniture, all with the same Art Nouveau ornamental forms and curving designs.

30. D: To create visual interest in this artwork, the artist Claude Monet arranged the still life asymmetrically. This is an effective method of creating a visually interesting composition. The arrangement does not form a pattern, nor does it use an analogous color scheme. The shapes used throughout the still life are primarily circles, seen in the various fruits spread out on the table.

31. C: Like oil paints, acrylic paints use toxic pigments and nontoxic pigments, depending on the colors being used by the artist. The artist must check each pigment to see how safe it is to use and what precautions they should take. Acrylic paints do dry much more quickly than oils, allowing the artist to work more quickly. Acrylics can be cleaned up with soap and water, and they can also be thinned with water, unlike oil paints.

32. B: An artist will often stretch watercolor paper prior to starting a painting, which will keep the paper from warping when water and paint are applied. One method is to soak it with water and then tape it to a board with a gummed paper tape. The paper is then allowed to dry overnight. When it dries, the paper stretches and will not warp when it is painted on. Alternately, an artist can buy a prestretched block of watercolor paper and peel each sheet off after using it.

33. A: Although an art gum eraser will also be gentle on the paper, the kneaded eraser is the only one that will not leave crumbs of eraser on the paper. A kneaded eraser can be molded to change its shape for various areas on a drawing, erasing small details and larger areas. It will not leave pieces behind, and it will not damage the paper. A pink pearl eraser, vinyl eraser, and art gum eraser will all leave crumbs of eraser behind on the paper when used.

34. A: Artwork in Ancient Egypt was mainly created for tombs and for a person's afterlife. Tombs were stockpiled with not only food and supplies, but also artwork and jewelry for a person's afterlife, especially for the wealthy. They used metals such as copper, gold, bronze, and silver, as well as stones including lapis lazuli, amethyst, quartz, and jasper for their jewelry. They also made carvings from a variety of native wood species.

35. B: It is important to correctly follow ethical standards involving copyright when creating artwork. If using other people's images, it is always important to read the fine print. It is best for the artist to use their own photographs or work from life. The artist should always get permission if using someone else's images or ideas and never copy someone else's artwork or ideas and present it as their own. If copying a famous work, it should be as an exercise only and not be placed for sale.

36. C: Art and sculpture from Africa include an emphasis on the human figure, as well as visual stylization rather than representing them naturalistically. African art also focuses on symmetry and geometry, and figures often emphasize physical strength and youthfulness, as shown in this sculpture. Although some African art, such as this sculpture, is made from bronze, other African sculpture and masks are made from wood.

37. D: Slip is a mix of clay and water that has a runny consistency. It is used to join pieces of clay by scoring the pieces and then applying the slip as a glue between them prior to joining. It can also be used to decorate ceramic pieces by brushing, dipping, spraying, or building up the slip in intricate designs onto the surface. Slip can even be used for casting in a mold, as a solid cast, or as a hollow cast depending on the purpose.

38. D: The Armory Show in 1913 was significant because it was the first major modern art show in America. It was also known as the International Exhibition of Modern Art, and it opened at the 69th Regiment Armory in New York City. Prior to this, Americans were accustomed to realistic and representational art and found this exhibition to be full of new, shocking, and exciting ideas. The exhibition was a huge success and showcased many well-known artists.

39. B: This image shows two-point perspective, in which two vanishing points are on the horizon line. In this case, the vanishing points would be on either side of the building, and the street and buildings would vanish into these vanishing points into the distance. The closest part of the building, from this perspective, is the front corner, and the horizon line is obscured by the buildings. The lines of the roof, ground, sidewalks, and windows could all be drawn back to the vanishing points.

40. A: The nave of a church is its center aisle, which usually extends from the main entrance to the apse or chancel. The apse or chancel is the vaulted, semicircular structure at the end of the aisle. A circular opening in the center of a dome is called an oculus, which is Latin for eye. A flat upright column inset in a wall is called a pilaster. It gives the appearance of a column without creating the same type of structural support that a column provides.

41. D: Enameling is a technique that involves melting powdered glass onto a surface at a heat of 750–850°C, which forms a shiny glass surface. This is often done on a metal surface, but enameling can also be done on glass or ceramic. The powdered glass is called frit, and it is colored by the addition of various minerals. Enameling can be transparent, opaque, or translucent once it is melted onto the surface.

42. D: Filigree is a metalworking technique that involves forming metal threads to create a lace pattern. The filigree technique requires skillful bending of wire to create simple or intricate patterns out of metal. The metal is first annealed prior to the filigree technique, which is a process of heating the metal and then cooling it slowly, to make it easier to work with. The basket in this image was created from many pieces of metal bent to form a delicate pattern.

43. B: A hot shoe on a camera is a mounting point where a flash would attach. It is a squared, U-shaped piece of metal with a metal contact point in the center. Modern cameras might have an accessory shoe without the function of creating an electrical circuit and will have the ability to be triggered wirelessly without using the contacts. A microphone, viewfinder, satellite positioning unit, or other accessories might be positioned at this point.

44. C: The context of an artwork is the conditions or circumstances around which it was created. This could include historical events; the environment in which the artist was working; the artist's background, traditions, and values; and other factors. The physical materials used by an artist to create artwork are called media. The ways in which an artist uses their skills to create a work are called techniques.

45. B: Up until the 1970s, the main genres accepted as fine art photography were nudes, landscapes, and portraits. In the early and mid-1900s, several photographers, including Ansel Adams, worked to advance the acceptance of photography as a fine art. Photographs had the potential to record detail, but they were also seen as a threat and shortcut to artwork, so their acceptance as fine art was a struggle for some time.

46. A: Mass tone is the color of a pigment straight from the tube of paint. This differs from the undertone of a paint, which is the color when applied thinly. A paint color can be very different when applied straight from the tube and applied thinly, or it can have the same characteristics. Some colors are naturally opaque, whereas others are naturally transparent. These characteristics all depend on the color's pigment.

47. D: If an oil painting is varnished too early, before the paint is completely dry, several things could happen. The varnish could crack, or it could turn tacky and not dry. If it is a matte varnish, it could sink and the matting agent could leave a white deposit on the paint surface. The varnish could sink into the paint and change the color of the paint. Any attempt to remove the varnish could also remove paint from the support.

48. A: During the Renaissance, artists would begin their career as an apprentice to a master artist. They would perform duties such as cleaning paintbrushes, grinding pigments, and preparing surfaces for paintings. They would slowly learn to sketch and transfer sketches to surfaces for frescoes and learn how to paint like their master artist. Communicating with patrons was left to the master artist, whereas apprentices performed lesser tasks.

49. C: After the ink is forced into the lines on the plate, the plate is wiped with a rag to remove the ink from the raised areas of the plate, leaving the ink only in the recessed lines and areas of the plate so that the plate is ready for printing. Then, the plate is placed onto the etching press, and a dampened sheet of etching paper is placed on the plate. Felt blankets are placed on top of the paper, and they are all run through the etching press between the steel rollers to create the print.

50. B: Willem de Kooning, Jackson Pollock, and Franz Kline are all associated with the Abstract Expressionism movement. This movement developed in New York in the 1940s, after World War II, and it was the first American movement to have international influence. Abstract Expressionist artists emphasized spontaneous and subconscious creation, gestural forms, abstraction, and emotion.

51. B: A tint of a color is a light value made by mixing a hue, or a color, with white. A shade, on the other hand, is a darker value made by mixing a hue or color with black. To make a tint of red, red would be mixed with white. A variety of tints could be made from red to white by mixing different amounts of red and white, just as a variety of shades could be made by mixing different amounts of red and black.

52. D: The horizon line is the line where the ground meets the sky in a landscape. When using this to create a perspective drawing, vanishing points are placed along the horizon line. The horizon line is also sometimes referred to as eye level, depending on the perspective used in an artwork. When using vanishing points, objects become smaller as they are closer to a vanishing point, and they are larger as they are farther away from a vanishing point.

53. C: A bas relief, or low-relief sculpture, is a sculpture that is attached to a slab or wall and projects only slightly from the surface. A high-relief sculpture, on the other hand, will project significantly from its attached slab or wall, and parts may even be detached from the surface. Neither a high- nor a low-relief sculpture is meant to be viewed from all sides, unlike a sculpture created in the round.

54. C: The Venuses were small Paleolithic sculptures made of stone and animal bone that depicted women with oversized stomachs and breasts and were likely fertility symbols. The most famous of these is the *Venus of Willendorf* found in Austria, c. 28,000–23,000 BC. The anatomy of the figure is exaggerated, the head is obscured with curly hair, and the anatomy seems to represent all of women, not just one woman, or possibly the idea of fertility.

55. A: A mihrab is a semicircular niche in a wall of a mosque, indicating the point in the mosque nearest to Mecca. This is used to indicate the direction to be faced when praying. Arabesque is an ornamental design used in Arabic artwork, using flowing lines and vines. It often covers a surface in a repeating pattern. A madrasa is a college for Islamic instruction, and a minbar is a short flight of steps used in a mosque by the preacher.

56. A: One of the reasons for the iconoclasm during the 700s in the Byzantine Empire was the belief that the Old Testament prohibited idolatry, and the Christian images depicted idols and should be banned as such. Iconoclasm refers to the destruction of these icons because of the hostility toward these representations for a number of reasons. This might have also been a way to restrain the growing wealth and power of the monasteries who produced these icons.

57. C: Proportion is the relationship of the sizes of various elements within an artwork. The way in which forms are organized in space is perspective. The line along which forms are organized in an artwork is the axis. The shape of the subject in an artwork is its form. Proportion deals with the difference between parts of a whole or the space between different elements of something such as a face.

58. D: The main difference between alkyds and traditional oil paints is that alkyds dry much more quickly than oil paints. Alkyds are compatible with oils, and they will have the same sheen, blending qualities, and thickness, but the drying time is much shorter. They will still give a longer working time than acrylics. Alkyds should not be layered over oil paints because the film will be less flexible and more likely to crack.

59. D: Gargoyles and grotesques will look similar and also have similar placement. The main difference between them is that the gargoyle will be functional with a waterspout whereas a grotesque is not functional and does not have a water spout. These can be stone carvings of fantastic or mythical creatures. Gargoyles are specifically designed to have a waterspout to convey water away from the side of a building.

60. D: Contrapposto, or "counterpose," is a pose that departs from a stiff and formal sculptural pose. Contrapposto is when a figure is putting its weight on one leg and has the other leg bent. The hips and shoulders are at opposite angles. This gives the figure a more dynamic, lifelike, and natural appearance. This was first used with Ancient Greek statues and was often used in Renaissance sculptures, including Michelangelo's *David.*

61. A: The artists of the New York School of the 1940s had many commonalities, including their age (except Hans Hofmann, who was in his fifties at the time). Many of them had worked on the WPA, or Works Progress Administration, prior to the New York School. They all believed in the individuality of the artist and had their own individual styles and theories of art. Due to this, they disagreed on styles and theories. For instance, Hofmann disliked surrealism, and de Kooning and Pollock used painting as a process of discovery.

62. B: Frank Stella removed expressive content from his artwork by eliminating visible brushstrokes, gesture, and definition of the surface. According to Stella, "... what you see is what you see." The viewer was not intended to read any other information into the artwork that wasn't there, and he reduced the artwork to the simplest form possible by detaching himself from his art and making the surface as flat as possible.

63. D: Gouache paint is often used for illustration due to its opacity and flat, matte sheen, its ability to be reworked with water, and its wide range of colors. Gouache is more opaque than watercolor, is thinner than acrylics, and comes in smaller tubes like watercolor paints. Gouache, watercolor, and acrylics are all water based, but only gouache and watercolor can be reworked with water once the paint has dried. Oil paint is oil based and cannot be mixed with water.

64. C: This statue of *Shiva as the Lord of Dance* is from the Chola Dynasty in India from c. 950–1000. Shiva is associated with dance and music and is often represented with a third eye, four arms, and a serpent around the neck. Shiva is a major deity of the Hindu religion, as part of the triumvirate including Brahma and Vishnu. Shiva's four arms represent the four cardinal directions, and Shiva has the weapon of a trident.

65. C: Exposure bracketing in photography means taking three photographs—one at the correct exposure, one underexposed, and one overexposed. With a digital camera with an automatic setting for exposure bracketing, this can be done automatically. This technique can be helpful in a difficult lighting situation, so the photographer will have the choice of several different exposures after the photographs have been taken.

66. B: A web graphic should have a small file size and load quickly. It does not need to have a high resolution for printing. A .jpg file does not have a transparency channel, so it must have a solid color background. A .gif image can have a transparent background, and it can be compressed to a small file, making it ideal for a web graphic. A .tif file can also be transparent, but it is a lossless raster format that is a larger size and not good for web publishing. A .raw file is also a large file by default.

67. A: A hake brush is a large, flat, oriental-style wash brush used to lay flat areas of color in a watercolor painting or ink wash. It has soft bristles, usually made from squirrel, goat, or ox hair. It could also be used for wetting the surface of the paper or for absorbing excess water from the paper. It would not be used for detail work or for any acrylic or oil painting. It would also not be used for egg tempera because egg tempera use requires small, short dabs of color that dry quickly.

68. D: Three English painters were credited with establishing watercolor painting as a credible artistic medium: Paul Sandby, Thomas Girtin, and Joseph Mallord William Turner. These men worked in watercolor in the late 18th century, and Sandby is credited as being the father of the English watercolor. William H. Bartlett was a 19th-century British topographical artist and illustrator who produced many engraved views of North American landscapes, but he was not among the English painters credited with establishing watercolor as an independent medium.

69. A: The United Nations Educational, Scientific, and Cultural Organization (UNESCO) has a program that preserves cultural heritage sites including the Taj Mahal, Stonehenge, and the Eiffel Tower. One stipulation is that the site must be man-made. A cultural heritage site protected by UNESCO must be an excellent example of settlement, architecture, or technology that represents a stage in human history.

70. D: This architectural element, with four sides and a pyramidal top, is an obelisk. The Washington Monument is an example of an obelisk. A caryatid is a stone carving, usually of the figure of a woman, used in place of a column as a support. An entablature is the horizontal lintel on a classical building that is above the columns and below the triangulated pediment. A peristyle is a row of columns lining a space such as a courtyard.

71. C: The traditional Japanese aesthetic of wabi-sabi is an acceptance of imperfections. It is shown in artwork through asymmetry, incompleteness, simplicity, and modesty. The simple, rustic forms of Japanese teaware embody the idea of wabi-sabi. This is also shown in clayware with asymmetry or unrefined finishing. Wabi-sabi can also suggest melancholy and solitude or serenity and beauty.

72. A: This critic would be using the formalism aesthetic theory to analyze this artwork. This is concerned primarily with how the artwork looks, including the use of elements and principles, and does not take into account the context or narrative related to the artwork. With this theory, all artwork would be approached and analyzed in the same way, so it is especially useful when analyzing non-representational and abstract artwork.

73. B: Rose windows, like mandalas, have radial symmetry. Rose windows are commonly found in Gothic cathedrals, and they can also be called wheel windows. They are divided into segments by spokes from a central point, much like a bicycle wheel. A rose window might have decorative stained glass, and it is often found in the nave or end of the transepts of a cathedral. Examples of these windows can be found all throughout Europe.

74. D: Thomas Cole, Albert Bierstadt, and Frederic Edwin Church were all painters of the Hudson River School, an American art movement in the mid-19th century. Hans Fredrik Gude was a painter in the Düsseldorf school of painting, which was a group of painters who studied at the Düsseldorf Academy in the 1830s and 1840s and inspired some of the Hudson River School painters. The Hudson River School focused on Romantic landscape paintings.

75. A: Still-life objects are usually grouped in odd amounts for visual interest; therefore, including three objects creates more visual interest than just two. Flattening the perspective of the table so that the objects do not look like they will slide off will ease some tension from this painting. It would also help if the bottoms of the rounded objects were more consistently rounded. Objects that are close together should either overlap or not touch at all rather than having "kissing" edges that barely touch.

76. B: Keith Haring was an American artist whose work focused on graffiti-styled chalk outlines. His subjects included babies, spaceships, dogs, as well as many political and social themes. Although he did use bright colors on often black or white backgrounds, his signature style was to use line to create his subjects and express his ideas. His drawings were flat and did not include texture, and they did not focus on using multiple values either.

77. A: Pattern and rhythm are both principles of design, but they differ in that pattern will repeat elements in the exact same order, whereas rhythm can repeat elements in a different order. The pattern can be of shapes, colors, lines, or other elements of art, and it can be in a line, a grid, or another arrangement. Either of these principles can be used to order and arrange elements within an artwork.

78. C: Philip Pearlstein is best known for creating photorealistic representations by painting from live models. He chose to work from life rather than photographs to capture accurate lighting and space for his artwork and paint what he sees in front of him rather than what is captured by a camera. His process is different from that of Chuck Close, who creates his photorealistic paintings using photographs and a grid system.

79. D: One of the themes that Cindy Sherman focused on in her photographic series was the various roles of women in society. She used photography to portray herself in various roles, including housewife, mother, and actress. By doing this, she was both herself and those characters, calling into question the concept of identity and how one woman could occupy various roles in society. She encourages society to examine the identities and roles of women.

80. C: If an artist is said to be a contemporary of another artist, it means that they lived at the same time as each other. People working during the same time are considered contemporaries. Artists working in the same style at the same time within the same group are contemporaries, but artists working in different styles in different groups at the same time are also considered contemporaries.

81. B: Appropriation involves taking an original idea or image and using it in a new or different context while it is still recognizable as the original image or object. Appropriation recontextualizes an image for a different purpose or different audience. Marcel Duchamp used the concept of appropriation when he took a premade urinal and presented it as artwork, signed "R. Mutt." Pop artists also often used appropriation to incorporate images from pop culture into their artwork.

82. A: The domes shown in this image are onion domes. These domes are wider than the base on which they sit, and they taper to a point at the top. The height is usually greater than the width. They are often found on Eastern Slavic churches, especially in Russia. They can also be found in Indo-Islamic architecture and in the Middle East and Central Asia. The onion domes on some cathedrals are brightly colored.

83. A: Surrealist artists were attempting to bypass reason and unlock ideas from the unconscious mind. Artists such as Salvador Dali and Rene Magritte sought to put these ideas down as artwork. Impressionist artists were trying to capture the effect of lighting on a scene. Cubist artists showed simultaneously interlocking planes used to construct a scene, and Dada artists were reacting against the bourgeois and departing from the traditional values of art.

84. D: Fine art is art that has a primary purpose of being aesthetically pleasing or intellectually stimulating. This can include paintings, drawings, and sculptures. Applied art is art that serves a purpose and might include graphic design, interior design, and architecture. Applied art can also include jewelry, ceramics, textiles, and other forms of art that are both decorative and serve a useful purpose. The line between fine art and applied art can be blurred depending on the intent of the creator.

85. D: A subtractive sculpture technique is one that starts with a large piece of material and the artist removes pieces to create the finished work. This is also known as carving, and it is commonly done with stone or wood. Michelangelo's *David,* carved from marble, is an example of the subtractive technique. An additive technique is any in which materials are added together to create the finished work, and this can be done with any number of materials.

86. C: Tempera paint, along with ink and gold foil, was used in illuminated manuscripts during the Middle Ages. Many different natural materials were used in creative ways to make the pigments and surfaces for these manuscripts. Parchments were crafted from animal skins, and colors were made from ultramarine, insects, nuts, and other materials that would lend their natural dyes to this artistry.

87. B: A tortillon is a tightly rolled piece of paper, tapered at one end, that is used for blending with pencil or charcoal. A blending stump is similar, but it is longer and is pointed at both ends. Using a tortillon can help the artist keep his or her fingers clean when blending drawing materials, and it can also help the artist achieve more control over blending because the tortillon has a finer point at the end.

88. A: Egg tempera was a popular medium until the 1500s when oil paints became more widely used. Although oil paint was used prior to the 1500s, it became more popular at this time and became the primary means of creating artwork, first on panels and then on canvas as canvas became more affordable and more readily available. Slow-drying oils helped Renaissance artists achieve the naturalism they sought.

89. B: It is recommended to remove all combustible materials from the kiln area before operating a kiln. Always unplug a kiln before working on the electrical components, and turn off the circuit breaker if it is hard wired. Use protective glasses if looking into the kiln for long periods of time. Do not unload the kiln before the temperature has dropped to at least 125°F. It is safer to allow the materials to cool slowly and unload them when they are cooler.

90. D: Repoussé is a metalworking technique that involves hammering a design into a malleable metal to create a low-relief design. The technique of chasing is used to refine this design on the front of the metal. Chasing is the opposite of repoussé. When used together, these two techniques are known as embossing. These techniques use the elasticity of the metal, and no metal is lost in the process.

91. A: A representation of the Virgin Mary holding the dead body of Christ is called a pietà. Michelangelo sculpted several pietàs throughout his life, including this example titled *Pietà,* which was carved from marble in 1498–1499. A predella is the lowest section of an altarpiece. A cassone is a traditional Italian marriage or hope chest. A campanile is a freestanding bell tower in Italian architecture.

92. C: Local color is the term for the true color of an object without the effect of light or shadow altering its appearance. When considering how to portray colors in artwork, an artist must understand the difference between local color and how light, shadow, atmosphere, and other factors can affect that color when making decisions about how to portray the color in their artwork. They will also need to decide whether to portray the color faithfully or alter the color scheme.

93. C: A figurative artwork is one that contains a recognizable subject, such as landscapes, people, animals, or still life. This is also called representational artwork, and it is clearly derived from real sources. This is in contrast to abstract art, which does not have a recognizable subject, and which might focus instead on color, shapes, form, and space rather than expressing the artist's ideas through the subject of the artwork.

94. D: Repoussoir is the deliberate framing of a two-dimensional work along a side so that the viewer's eye is directed toward the center. This is a compositional choice made by the artist, and in a landscape painting, it might include branches or other landscape elements framing the artwork. In an artwork involving architecture, the framing could include columns or arches. In an interior, it could consist of a wall, archway, or curtain.

95. B: A registration mark is used in graphic design so that the printer can line up multiple printing plates. When a graphic is printed using CMYK, for example, each color will need to be aligned so that the colors overlap precisely for the final image. The registration mark is a check to see that all colors are aligned correctly. The registration mark is printed outside of the area of the final work and will be trimmed away from the final piece.

96. A: The artists of the Pointillism movement relied heavily on optical color mixing. They would place small dots of colors next to each other and allow the brain to involuntarily mix the colors rather than mixing the colors on their palette. The Pointillism movement was pioneered by Georges Seurat, who experimented with juxtaposition of colors. Other prominent artists of this movement included Paul Signac and Camille Pissarro.

97. C: A siccative is an agent that is added to an oil or varnish to shorten its drying time. Sinopia is a reddish-brown underpainting created prior to a fresco, some of which have been found to be quite different from the final fresco. Retardataire describes an artwork created with a seeming lack of awareness of other styles of that time. Trucage is the forgery of a painting, and a person who forges a painting is a truqueur.

98. B: Cerography, also called glyphography, is a printmaking method in which an image is carved into a layer of wax that has been applied to a metal surface. A positive plate is then created through a method of electrotyping or stereotyping, and the plate can then be used for printing. This method was developed in the 1830s and was intended mainly to reproduce line drawings and maps because it was not able to recreate shading.

99. D: The Aesthetic movement rebelled against Victorian ideals and sought to create "art for art's sake." Artists emphasized quality craftsmanship and art as a part of everyday life. The artists of this movement embraced all forms of art, including fine arts and crafts. They pursued beauty in form and color, independent of any message or agenda. Prominent artists of this movement included James Abbott McNeill Whistler and Dante Gabriel Rossetti.

100. A: The four stages of art criticism are description, analysis, interpretation, and judgment. Description involves noticing what we see within the artwork. Analysis involves scrutinizing the formal qualities, elements, and principles within an artwork. Interpretation involves trying to understand what the artist is attempting to communicate through the artwork. Judgment involves deciding whether the artwork is successful.

Practice Test #2

1. Which of the following best describes a fugitive pigment?

a. A pigment that tends to run or drip off of a canvas
b. A pigment that changes qualities when exposed to environmental conditions
c. A pigment that has lasted throughout many centuries without change
d. A pigment that is difficult to locate sources for its creation

2. Which of the following color systems is considered a subtractive color system?

a. CMYK
b. RGB
c. HSV
d. ROYGBIV

3. Which of the following best describes putti in Renaissance artwork?

a. Groupings of fruit shown in still life paintings
b. Depictions of naked, chubby male children, sometimes with wings
c. A hazy quality created by gradually blending tones together
d. A perspective effect created by shortening lines

4. Which of the following art movements was the Der Blaue Reiter movement most closely related to?

a. Neo-Expressionism
b. Les Nabis
c. German Expressionism
d. Dada

5. This statue is an example of which period of Greek sculpture?

a. Archaic
b. Classical
c. Hellenistic
d. Geometric

6. An artist creates a sculpture from found objects, similar to a three-dimensional collage. Which of the following is the correct term for this sculpture method?

a. Construction
b. Arrangement
c. Fabrication
d. Assemblage

7. Which of the following art movements does this work exemplify?

a. Romanticism
b. Neoclassicism
c. Rococo
d. Baroque

8. Which of the following is the correct term for a brownish-red, porous, earthenware clay?

a. Terra cotta
b. Porcelain
c. Raku
d. Kaolin

9. Which of the following describes a computer graphics term for smoothing the edges of images to minimize distortion?

a. Planing
b. Antialiasing
c. Leveling
d. Trimming

10. Which of the following is the correct term for these dots that are placed at various sizes to create a gradient effect?

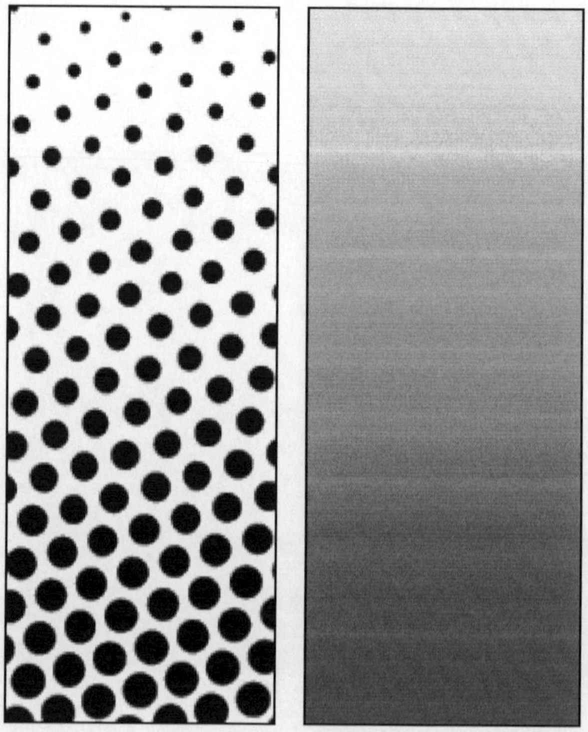

a. Dither
b. Rasterization
c. Halftone
d. Ben-Day dots

11. Which of the following would NOT be a part of an entablature in Classical Greek architecture?

a. Architrave
b. Frieze
c. Cornice
d. Pediment

12. Which of the following was the first type of photograph invented by Niépce around 1824?

a. Heliograph
b. Calotype
c. Cyanotype
d. Daguerreotype

13. Which of the following is NOT a reason for using an underpainting technique in a painting?

a. To build up textures for an artwork
b. To lay out the highlights and shadows for an artwork
c. To establish the tones for an artwork
d. To build the foundation for the colors of the artwork

14. Which of the following best describe the Ancient Egyptians' attitude toward art?

a. Art emphasized the idea that all people were equal in the afterlife, regardless of their role on earth.
b. Art highlighted the youth and vitality of warriors in their culture.
c. Art expressed emotion, and it was meant to show the beauty of the world.
d. Art was functional, provided an idealized view of the world, and maintained order.

15. Which of the following is a criticism of some environmental art, including Robert Smithson's "Spiral Jetty"?

a. Environmental art should not be categorized as art.
b. Environmental art should include other artistic media.
c. Environmental art can neglect to focus on environmental issues.
d. Environmental art can permanently damage the land it was created on.

16. Which of the following colors can the phthalocyanine pigment be found in?

a. Red and yellow
b. Blue and green
c. Yellow and green
d. Blue and violet

17. The dots that Roy Lichtenstein used in his comic-style artwork were named after which of the following people?

a. Shepard Fairey
b. Benjamin Henry Day Jr.
c. Milton Glaser
d. Saul Bass

18. Which of the following best describes the motivation of the Deconstructivism architectural movement?

a. To undermine preconceived notions of meaning and symbols
b. To incorporate natural materials within the creation of a structure
c. To recall the styles and traditions of the classical era
d. To break down elements into their most basic geometric parts

19. Which of the following best describes Le Corbusier's attitude toward designing living spaces?

a. People should be allowed easy contact with the nature around them.
b. People should have a tightly regimented living space that provides only for their basic needs.
c. People should have an open, unencumbered living space to decorate and design as they desire.
d. People should have a functional living space, providing for all their physical and psychosomatic needs.

20. Which of the following describes the point of view used by the artist in this artwork?

a. Bird's-eye view
b. Eye level view
c. Worm's-eye view
d. Open view

21. Which of the following best describes iconography in regard to an artwork?

a. Iconography is what a work is about.
b. Iconography is the style of the work.
c. Iconography is the artist's intention.
d. Iconography is the context of the work.

22. Which of the following situations would NOT fall under fair use provisions of US copyright law when using an image?

a. Using an image for educational purposes
b. Using another artist's entire image for resale purposes
c. Repurposing and recontextualizing an image to create new meaning
d. Using a small part of a copyrighted image in a class project

23. Which of the following would be the correct method of making a shade of the color blue?

a. Adding white to blue
b. Adding black to blue
c. Adding red to blue
d. Adding green to blue

24. Which of the following best describes the fiber art technique of macramé?

a. Looping material with a hooked needle
b. Interlacing long threads on a loom to create a large piece of fabric
c. Combining fibers to make a thread or a yarn
d. Tying knots in a thread or cord in a geometric pattern

25. Which of the following best describes the goal of East Asian sumi-e brush painting?

a. To faithfully reproduce the details of a subject
b. To recreate the colors of a subject
c. To capture the spirit of a subject
d. To replicate the contours of a subject

26. Which of the following is true about photographs such as this one taken by Civil War photographer Matthew Brady?

a. The subjects of the photograph were often moved and staged for a better composition.
b. Brady did not acquire permission to take these photographs on the battlefield.
c. The dead shown in these photos were often live subjects pretending to be dead for the photographs.
d. Brady took all of the photographs himself, without the help of an assistant.

27. Which of the following groups of colors could be classified as warm colors?

a. Red, yellow, and orange
b. Red, yellow and blue
c. Blue, green, and violet
d. Orange, green, and violet

28. Which of the following best describes representation in artwork?

a. Combining different styles in one image
b. Using colors creatively
c. Depicting objects in a faithful manner
d. Using signs that stand for something else

29. Which of the following elements does artist Helen Frankenthaler most focus on in her artwork?

a. Line
b. Color
c. Texture
d. Form

30. Which of the following is NOT known to be a highly toxic pigment?

a. Manganese violet
b. Cobalt yellow
c. Cadmium red hue
d. Chrome orange

31. Which of the following best describes the deckle as it relates to the papermaking process?

a. A screen used to drain the water away from the paper slurry
b. The fiber that is combined to create the paper pulp
c. A wooden frame used to control the size of the sheet of paper
d. The lines made by the screen when the paper dries

32. Which of the following best describes the motivation behind the artwork of the Guerrilla Girls?

a. To gain acceptance for women's right to vote
b. To include more images of women in artwork in museums
c. To create separate spaces for women's artwork
d. To speak out against racism and sexism in the art world

33. Which of the following best describes the term *icon* as it relates to artwork?

a. A religious painting, usually of one or two subjects
b. An artwork of an arrangement of objects, usually fruit or flowers
c. A painting of a person, usually just of the head and shoulders
d. An artwork of an outdoor scene

34. If viewing this artwork as foreground, middle ground, and background, which of the following elements would be considered the middle ground?

a. The reclining man
b. The mountains
c. The tree
d. The man herding two cows

35. This image is an example of which of the following artistic rendering techniques?

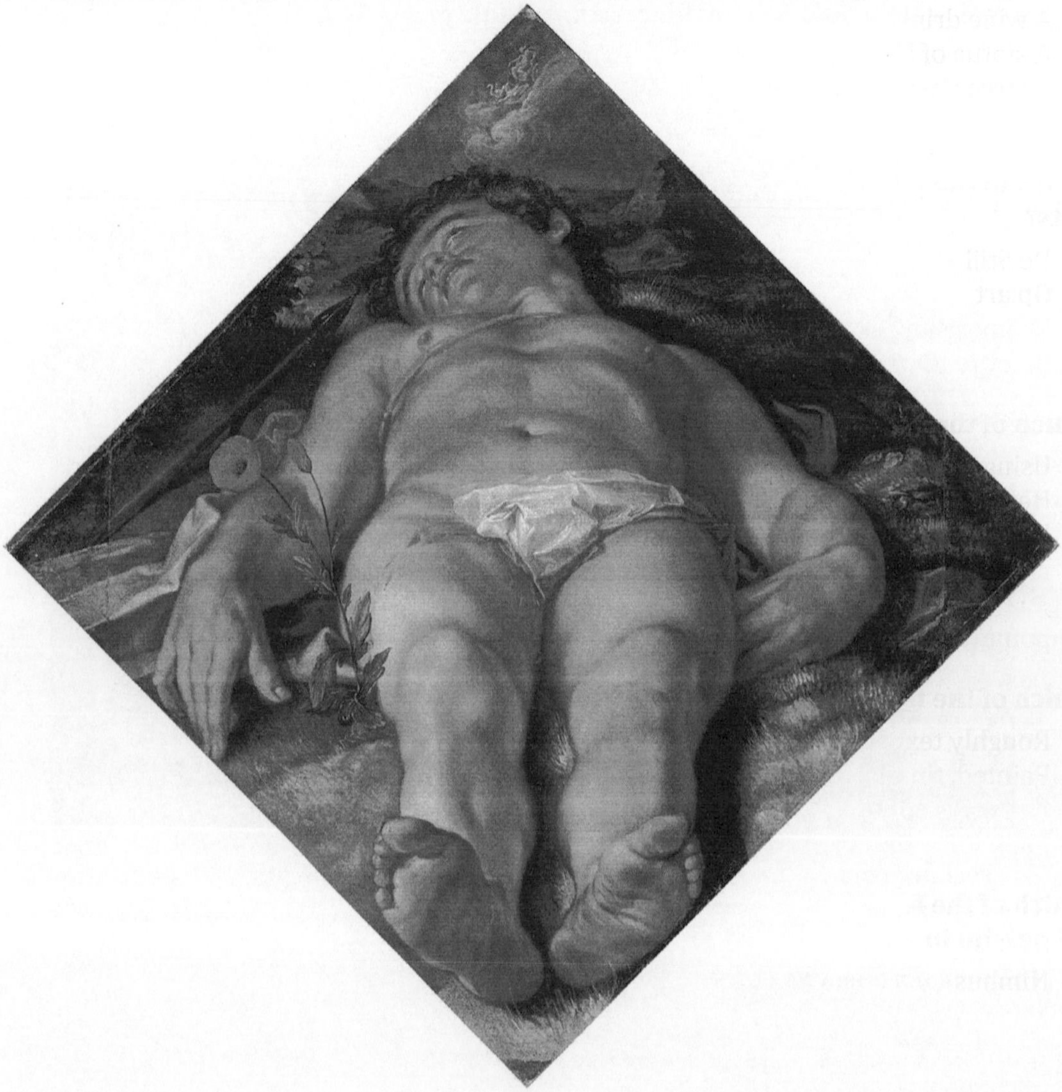

a. Foreshortening
b. Vanishing point
c. Golden mean
d. Chiaroscuro

36. A graphic designer needs to send files to a printer for a high-resolution brochure project. Which of the following file formats should the graphic designer NOT send?

a. .psd
b. .pdf
c. .tif
d. .png

37. Which of the following best describes a kylix?

a. A wine drinking cup that is wide and shallow
b. A statue of a young boy, standing tall and symmetrically
c. A large vase used to water down wine
d. A tall jar with a narrow neck and two handles

38. Which of the following art movements would be more likely to include figurative subjects?

a. De Stijl
b. Op art
c. Mannerism
d. Color field

39. Which of the following best describes the metalworking technique of brazing?

a. Using high heat to melt two or more adjoining metal items together
b. Heating two or more metal items to a high heat and then hammering them together
c. Joining two or more metal items by melting and flowing a filler metal with a lower melting point than the adjoining metal
d. Joining two or more metal items by melting and flowing a filler metal with a higher melting point than the adjoining metal

40. Which of the following best describes azulejos used in architecture?

a. Roughly textured, hand-applied mix of cement, water, sand, or lime
b. Painted, tin-glazed ceramic tiles used to embellish walls, floors, and ceilings
c. Red clay roof tiles
d. Functional tower-like chimneys

41. Which of the following is NOT a type of representation of an emanation of light around a sacred person in an artwork?

a. Nimbus
b. Mandorla
c. Aureole
d. Gisant

42. Which of the following drawing techniques, used in the 15th and 16th centuries on a specially coated paper, is shown here?

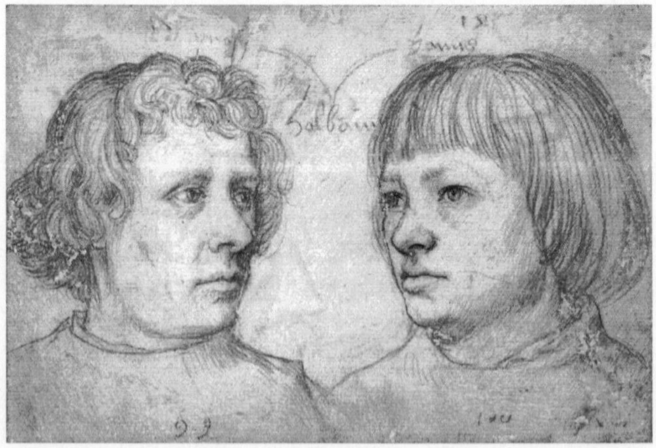

a. Silver point
b. Conté crayon
c. Charcoal
d. Graphite

43. A building is being returned as nearly as possible to its original condition. Which of the following terms most closely applies to this process?

a. Renovation
b. Conservation
c. Preservation
d. Restoration

44. Which of the following pigments was NOT available to Paleolithic artists?

a. Yellow
b. Blue
c. Brown
d. Black

45. Which of the following best describes a pagoda?

a. A tall, four-sided stone pillar with a pyramidal top
b. A small, dome-like structure on the top of a building
c. A multistory tower with multiple eaves, found in South or East Asia
d. A rectangular, terraced temple in ancient Mesopotamia

46. Which of the following periods of Greek sculpture was known for focusing on naturalism and expressive movement when portraying the human figure?

a. Geometric
b. Archaic
c. Hellenistic
d. Classical

47. Which of the following best describes outsider art?

a. Art created by self-taught artists outside of the mainstream art world
b. Art created with natural materials in the outdoor environment
c. Art created by artists who have not been allowed to join an art movement
d. Art created en plein air, or in the natural light

48. Which of the following art movements did NOT fight against the commodification of art?

a. Pop Art
b. Performance art
c. Conceptual art
d. Earth art

49. A member of which of the following groups of artists created this artwork?

a. Cobra Group
b. Ashcan School
c. Les Fauves
d. Hudson River School

50. Which of the following best describes the fiber arts practice of tatting?

a. Making interlocking loops of yarn with a hook
b. Decorative sewing using a needle
c. Using a needle or shuttle to create lace with knots and loops
d. Using needles to create multiple stitches of yarn in a line

51. If an artist creates a pastiche, which of the following best describes what they are creating?

a. A decorative motif based on a palm leaf
b. A small model as a trial sketch for a larger sculpture
c. An artwork created in three panels
d. A work of art in the style of another artist

52. Which of the following best describes the focus of the Fluxus art movement?

a. Cynicism and antirational artwork, with appropriation and a rethinking of the concept of art
b. Idealizing the working class and making artwork accessible to everyone
c. Conceptual performances and emphasis on the process rather than on the product
d. Juxtaposing dots of pure color for optical color mixing

53. Which of the following best describes gesso?

a. A stick of colored material bound with gum arabic and used for drawing
b. A paint containing gypsum, pigment, or chalk that is used for preparing a surface for painting
c. An inexpensive, opaque form of watercolor containing fugitive pigments
d. A sizing that also acts as a glue, created from refined collagen

54. Which of the following is the correct term for a distorted drawing, such as the following example, that only looks optically correct when viewed with a mirror or lens?

a. Algraphy
b. Antiphonary
c. Anamorphosis
d. Antependium

55. Which of the following theories of art criticism is the most straightforward for critiquing modern artwork, by analyzing the visual aspects of the artwork?

a. Formalism
b. Expressionism
c. Deconstructivism
d. Representationalism

56. Which of the following critical responses was directed at the Minimalist art movement?

a. It undervalued art by blurring the line between art and everyday objects.
b. It did not contain enough color to qualify as artwork.
c. Artwork without representational subjects does not count as art.
d. Critics were not able to critique it with any of the art criticism theories.

57. Which of the following best describes the architectural element spandrel?

a. The middle part of an entablature, between the cornice and architrave
b. An ornamental molding common on facades
c. A stylized leaf used as a decorative motif
d. The triangular area between the outer curve of an arch and the framework

58. Which of the following is the term for the method shown of portraying heads in an artwork all at the same height, regardless of posture?

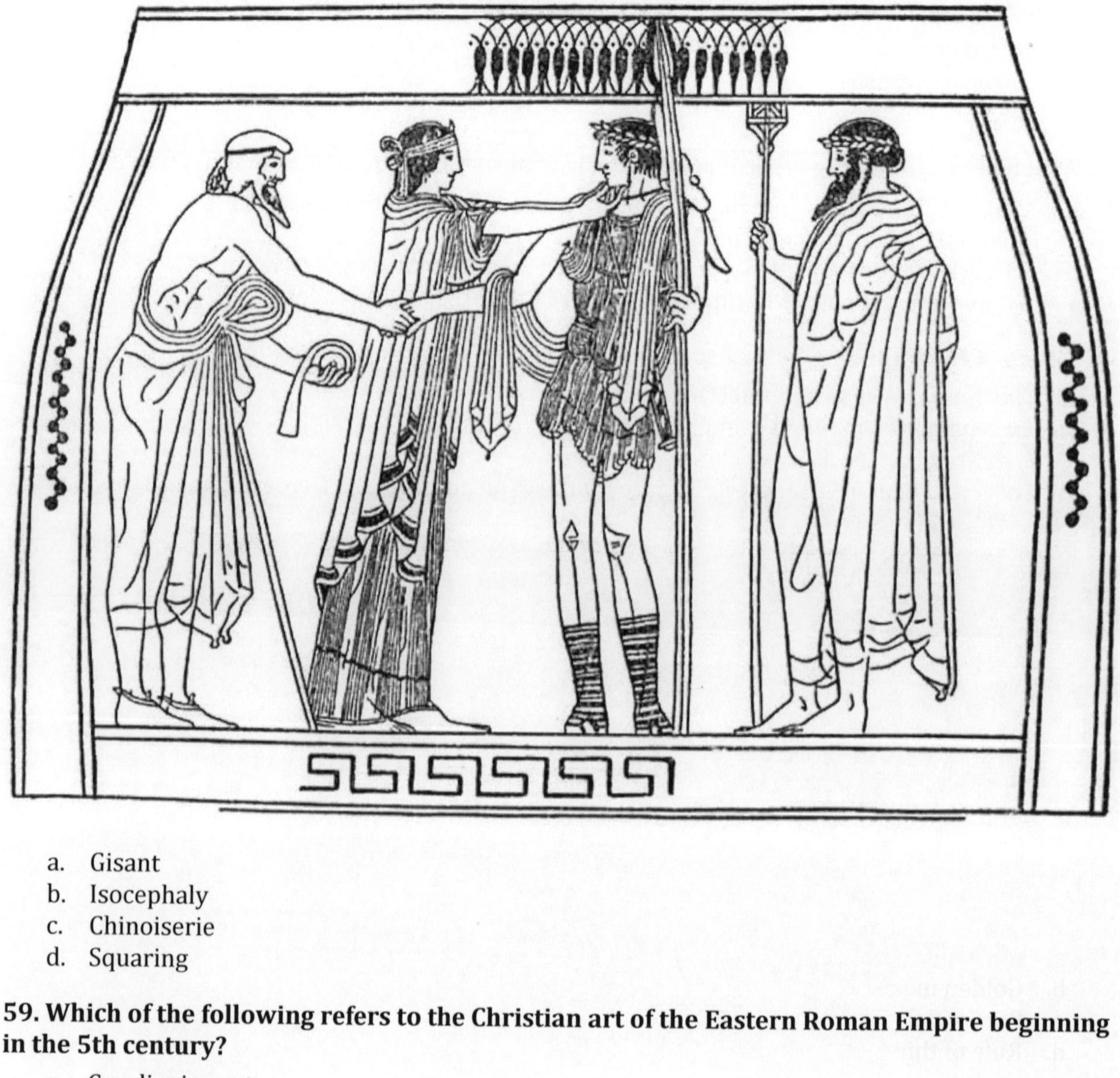

a. Gisant
b. Isocephaly
c. Chinoiserie
d. Squaring

59. Which of the following refers to the Christian art of the Eastern Roman Empire beginning in the 5th century?

a. Carolingian art
b. Byzantine art
c. Etruscan art
d. Ottonian art

60. Which of the following compositional techniques is being used in this painting?

a. Baroque composition
b. Golden mean
c. Pyramidal composition
d. Rule of thirds

61. An artist wants to use a white oil paint for glazing. Which of the following pigments would be best suited for this?

a. Zinc white
b. Flake white
c. Titanium white
d. Cremnitz white

62. Which of the following best describes the sculpture technique of casting?

a. A material is built up, sometimes over an armature.
b. Different materials are gathered and put together.
c. Pieces of a material are carved or chipped away.
d. A material is melted down, and then it is poured into a mold.

63. Which of the following best describes the oil painting technique of scumbling?

a. Applying a glaze over a light area to create a shadow
b. Using a tool to scratch through a layer of paint while it is still damp
c. Applying a thin layer of an opaque color over an area to produce a softened effect
d. Creating very gradual transitions between dark and light for a smoky effect

64. Which of the following is another term for a watercolor painting?

a. Aquarelle
b. Aquatint
c. Aquamanile
d. Aquagraph

65. Which of the following best describes how the realism movement rejected the ideas of Romanticism?

a. Realism preferred to portray people heroically and sentimentally, rather than in unpleasant scenes.
b. Realism rejected heightened emotions and exaggerated scenes, preferring to portray accuracy and truth.
c. Realism showed the monarchy in the best possible light, rejecting the portrayal of everyday scenes.
d. Realism depicted the rich and poor living on the same level, rejecting the idea of social hierarchy.

66. Which of the following best describes characteristics of Bauhaus architecture?

a. Enclosed courtyards, arches, domes, and arcades
b. Steel frames, open floor plans, and primary colors
c. Columns, grandeur of scale, and clean lines
d. Horseshoe arches, perforated screens, and geometric designs

67. Which of the following principles of design is most evident in this painting?

a. Balance
b. Contrast
c. Emphasis
d. Rhythm

68. Which of the following is the correct term for art that moves, driven by forces of nature, magnets, motors, or other outside forces?

a. Kinetic
b. Dynamic
c. Magnetic
d. Agile

69. Which of the following best describes the tintype process?

a. A direct positive image is made on a thin plate of metal.
b. An image is created on a silvered copper plate.
c. An image is created on paper coated in silver iodide.
d. An image is created on a piece of glass.

70. Which of the following best describes the greenware stage of clay?

a. Clay that is partially dry but not completely dry
b. Clay that has been fired once but is still porous
c. Clay that has been shaped and dried but not fired yet
d. Clay that is still soft and easily worked

71. Which of the following describes a benefit of dry mounting artwork?

a. It is easily removable if the artwork needs to be removed from the backing.
b. It uses a uniform coat of adhesive to keep the artwork from slumping in the frame.
c. Dry mounting is considered archival.
d. It is an inexpensive way to mount artwork.

72. An artist wants to create a loose, sketchy gesture drawing. Which of the following would NOT be the best choice for this type of drawing?

a. Conté crayon
b. 4H pencil
c. Vine charcoal
d. Soft pastel

73. In this landscape by Thomas Cole, which of the following best describes the term sublime as it applies to the mood of the painting?

a. Drama and emotion
b. Awe in the face of greatness and beauty
c. Love and absolute power
d. Sadness and a sense of despair

74. Which of the following best describes the term transformation as it relates to artwork?

a. Placing an object next to a contrasting object to emphasize it
b. Using unusual proportion to call attention to an object
c. Using preexisting images or objects with little or no changes
d. Changing an object and presenting it in a new way

75. Which of the following types of perspective is used to portray buildings shown from above or below?

a. One-point perspective
b. Two-point perspective
c. Three-point perspective
d. Four-point perspective

76. Which of the following describes the printmaking process of manière criblée?

a. The design is punched into a metal plate, creating a white spotted background.
b. The artist draws or paints on a smooth, nonabsorbent surface.
c. Material is cut off of a sheet of linoleum or wood to create a design.
d. Lines are cut into a sheet of metal to create a design.

77. Which of the following best describes the form of this sculpture?

a. An open, dynamic form, composed of organic shapes
b. A closed, dynamic form, composed of geometric shapes
c. An open, static form, with no interior contours
d. A closed, static form with exterior contours

78. Which of the following is the correct term for the rigid frame that a sculptor might use within a sculpture?

a. Maquette
b. Armature
c. Minaret
d. Iconoclast

79. Which of the following best describes the concept of composition in an artwork?

a. The presentation of shapes in a work of art
b. The subject matter of a work of art
c. How form is organized in a work of art
d. The range of colors used in a work of art

80. Which of the following is the tool used to draw lines in hot wax when using a batik technique?

a. Cassone
b. Cornice
c. Colonette
d. Canting

81. How did the creator of this mask use a principle of design to organize an element of art?

a. Rhythm to organize value
b. Pattern to organize line
c. Emphasis to organize space
d. Movement to organize shape

82. Which of the following best describes the function of an image sensor on a digital camera?

a. Converting the information of the image into an electronic signal
b. Changing the size of the lens opening
c. Storing the image information
d. Where light enters the camera

83. Which of the following does NOT describe a way that the advent of oil paints affected the use of egg tempera as a medium?

a. Artists used egg tempera as an underpainting for oil paintings.
b. Artists combined an egg yolk and oil emulsion called tempera grassa.
c. Artists' use of egg tempera versus oils was well documented.
d. Artists switched back and forth between both media.

84. Which of the following describes an advantage of lossy file compression for images?

a. The size of the file is reduced, but the file is still recognizable.
b. Unnecessary metadata are removed, but the file can still be used.
c. The file can be emailed and is now pixelated.
d. Quality is lost, and the image resolution becomes lower.

85. During which of the following time periods would panel paintings have been most prevalent?

a. Baroque
b. Mannerism
c. Neoclassical
d. Middle Ages

86. Which of the following best describes this example of photo retouching?

a. The man was removed from this photo for aesthetic purposes.
b. The man was removed from this photo for political purposes.
c. The man was removed from this photo for ethical purposes.
d. The man was removed from this photo for historical purposes.

87. An art critic describes an artwork based solely on its context within the art world. Which theory is this critic using?

a. Formalism
b. Institutional
c. Expressionism
d. Deconstruction

88. Which of the following best describes the term tessellation?

a. A continuous landscape painting around the walls of a room
b. Decorative painting used to replicate the look of marble or other finishings
c. The tiling of a shape potentially infinitely with no overlaps or gaps
d. A network of hairline cracks found in aged paintings and ceramics

89. Which of the following best describes a triadic color scheme?

a. Three colors evenly spaced on the color wheel
b. One color plus the two adjacent to its complement
c. Three adjacent colors on the color wheel
d. Three colors within the same color family (warm or cool)

90. Which of the following is the LEAST likely way to display a stone sculpture?

a. On a pedestal
b. In a glass display case
c. On the ground
d. Hung on the wall

91. Which of the following is the correct term for this device that projects an image through a small hole as an inverted image?

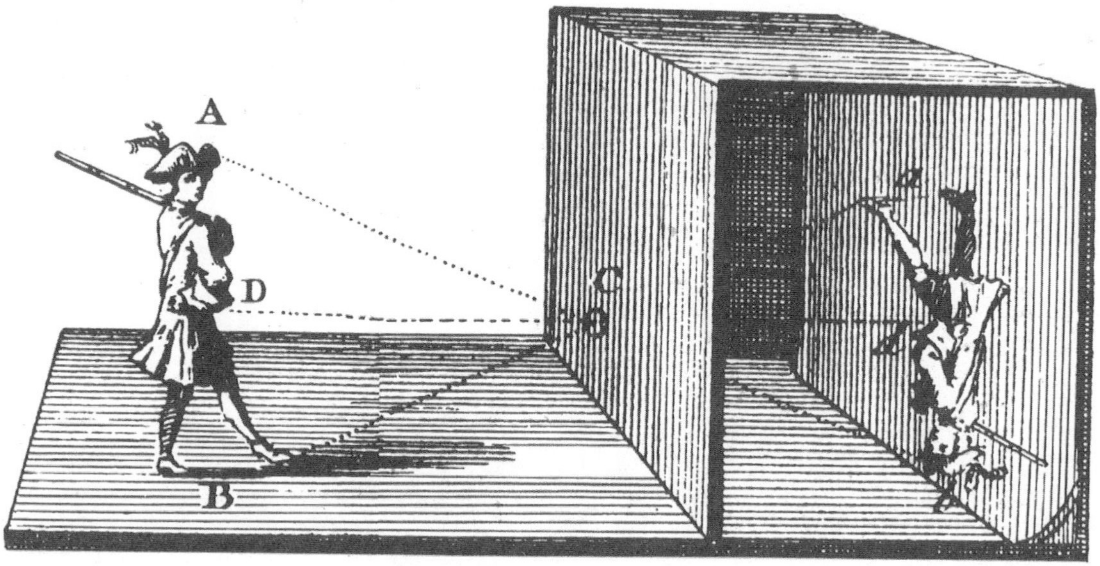

a. Daguerreotype
b. Stereoscope
c. Camera obscura
d. Calotype

92. Which of the following is NOT a common safety concern when using a spray can?

a. Inhalation of the solvent in sprayed paint
b. Dust creating chronic lung problems
c. Inhalation of pigments in sprayed paint
d. Flammable propane and propellants contained in aerosol spray paints

93. Which of the following best describes the medium encaustic?

a. Paint made from pigment mixed with gum arabic
b. Paint made from pigment mixed with a drying oil, usually linseed
c. Paint made from pigment added to heated beeswax
d. Paint made from pigment added to acrylic polymer emulsion

94. Which of the following is NOT a standard frame size for presenting artwork for display?

a. 10″ × 20″
b. 11″ × 14″
c. 8″ × 10″
d. 16″ × 20″

95. Which of the following best describes a periodic, or intermittent, kiln?

a. The ware is loaded into cars and slowly brought through the kiln on rails while the kiln is kept at a constant temperature.
b. The kiln is opened, loaded, and unloaded while already at its desired temperature.
c. The ware is loaded into cars and slowly brought through the kiln on rails and the kiln is brought up to the desired temperature.
d. The kiln is loaded, brought up to its desired temperature, cooled, then unloaded.

96. Which of the following categories would this artwork best fit under?

a. Color field art
b. Op art
c. Minimalist art
d. Pop Art

97. Which of the following best describes the reason for applying sizing to a canvas prior to painting?

a. To create a blank white surface to begin a painting on
b. To protect the canvas from the acids within the paints
c. To stiffen the canvas so that it is easier to paint on
d. To shrink the canvas slightly to tighten the wooden stretchers

98. Which of the following would be considered a modern sculpture material?

a. Stainless steel
b. Bronze
c. Marble
d. Stoneware

99. Which of the following best describes the difference between form in two- and three-dimensional artwork?

a. In two-dimensional artwork, form consists of geometric shapes, but in three-dimensional artwork, it can include organic shapes.
b. In two-dimensional artwork, form can be repeated, but in three-dimensional artwork, it is not.
c. In two-dimensional artwork, form consists of the dimensions of the paper or canvas, but in three-dimensional artwork, it is the size of the sculpture.
d. In two-dimensional artwork, form has width and height, but in three-dimensional artwork, it also has depth.

100. Which of the following terms describes the relationship of the size of the central figure to the surrounding figures in this image?

a. Golden proportion
b. Inaccurate proportion
c. Hierarchical proportion
d. Compositional proportion

Answer Key and Explanations for Test #2

1. B: A fugitive pigment is an impermanent pigment that changes over time with exposure to environmental conditions such as light, heat, cold, pollution, and humidity. Fugitive pigments can be found in markers, paints, inks, and other art media, and they may be used purposely for temporary applications. Paints that are more likely to have longevity have permanence and lightfastness ratings to tell the artist how durable the pigment will be over time.

2. A: CMYK is a subtractive color system because the pigments absorb some wavelengths of light, but not others, and they "subtract" the colors green, red, and blue from white light. White minus green, red, and blue gives us cyan, magenta, and yellow. The additive system includes red, green, and blue (RGB), and it works by adding red, green, and blue in various ways to create a wide array of colors through light, such as on television screens or computers.

3. B: Putti are chubby, naked male children depicted in Renaissance artwork, sometimes shown with wings. The singular of putti is putto. Although these were often found in Renaissance artwork, they originally came from sarcophagi in the 2nd century, and they were also depicted in the Baroque and Mannerist periods as well. Cupid was often depicted as a putto, and putti were depicted along with humans in many artworks.

4. C: The Der Blaue Reiter movement was one of the two pioneering movements of German Expressionism, along with Die Brücke. Der Blaue Reiter was a group of German artists who created abstract art and promoted the expression of spirituality in artwork. This group created work from 1911–1914, and it included artists such as Wassily Kandinsky, August Macke, Franz Marc, and Paul Klee.

5. A: This sculpture is an example of the Archaic period of Greek sculpture, which lasted from 650–500 BC. The Archaic period is characterized by a stiff and formal pose, similar to Egyptian statues. The standing nude male youth, a common subject, was called kouros. They were broad shouldered and narrow waisted, had their hands clenched at their sides, and had a slight, closed-mouth smile.

6. D: An assemblage is a sculpture method that involves putting together, or assembling, various pieces that might include found objects. This method originated with Pablo Picasso, and it has been used by artists including Robert Rauschenberg and Louise Nevelson. The origin of the term dates back to Jean Dubuffet's collages of butterfly wings from the 1950s, which he titled *assemblages d'empreintes.*

7. A: Eugene Delacroix's *Liberty Leading the People* (1830) is one of the best-known examples of Romantic history painting. Romanticism also calls to mind vast and awe-inspiring landscapes, such as those painted by the Hudson River School. Romanticism was a movement not only in art, but also in literature and music from about 1800 to 1850. It glorified nature and the past, and it emphasized feelings and emotion, causing artists to create awe-inspiring and grand artworks.

8. A: Terra cotta is a brownish-red, earthenware clay. It is used for sculptural purposes as well as utilitarian purposes including tiles, pots, bricks, and pipes. It is porous after being fired, and it can be glazed or can be left unglazed. In ancient times, terra cotta sculptures and other wares were left in the sun to dry. When kilns were used later, this clay was fired to 600–1000°C, and the iron content of the clay would give the piece its reddish color.

9. B: Antialiasing is a term for techniques used to smooth the edges of graphics to minimize distortion. This might be used when presenting a graphic at a lower resolution, and it smooths the jagged edges. In addition to images, antialiasing can also be used in the graphics of games to diminish jagged edges and make graphics look more realistic. At higher resolutions, the amount of antialiasing that is needed decreases.

10. C: Halftone is a graphic technique in which dots are created in various sizes to create a gradient effect. This can be done with black-and-white images by using black dots only, or it can be done with color images by overlaying CMYK dots and using them in combination. The transparency of the inks creates an optical effect that allows the colors to blend when printed together, allowing the finished image to look realistic.

11. D: The pediment is the triangular element that is situated atop the horizontal entablature in Classical Greek architecture. The entablature consists of the cornice, directly below the pediment, then the frieze, and the architrave, which is above the columns. In the Doric order, the frieze may be divided into triglyphs and metopes.

12. A: Nicéphore Niépce developed the first photographic technique, called heliography. This technique took anywhere from eight hours to several days of exposure, and the initial results were coarse. After this, Louis Daguerre developed the daguerreotype, which became the first commercially available photographic process. This was a great advancement, as it required a much shorter exposure and produced better results than the heliograph.

13. A: Underpainting is a technique used to create a thin layer that is a base for a finished painting, and it can be used to establish tone, darks and lights, and colors as a base for the final artwork. It is not used to build up textures. The underpainting layer is done in a thin layer to dry quickly and to serve as a base for the painting, almost as a sketch underneath the painting to establish where everything will go.

14. D: For Ancient Egyptians, art was functional, provided an idealized view of the world, and maintained order. Portraying an object in artwork gave it permanence, and the Ancient Egyptians used this concept to portray their own idealistic view of the world. They stylized people, used hierarchical proportion to designate importance, and they used colors and symbols to establish their own symbolism throughout their artwork, leaving a legacy of what was important to them.

15. D: A criticism of some environmental art, including Smithson's "Spiral Jetty," is that it can permanently damage the land on which it was created. Environmental art is considered art, although it is difficult to exhibit in a gallery as-is, and usually this is done by displaying photos of the artwork. It will often focus on environmental issues, and it does contain parts of the surrounding environment to create the artwork.

16. B: Phthalocyanine is a pigment that is found in blue and green paints. It is a bright synthetic pigment with a brilliant coloring in paints and dyes, and it has a high lightfastness rating, high tinting strength, and superior covering power. Phthalocyanine is a strong pigment that is insoluble in water. In paints, this color makes a strong glaze when diluted, while keeping its color intensity. Phthalo blue paint can be found in a red shade or a green shade.

17. B: Ben-Day dots are named after Benjamin Henry Day Jr., who was an illustrator and printer. He was the son of a 19th-century publisher, and he developed this process that distributes dots of an equal size throughout an area in the four process colors: cyan, magenta, yellow, and black. These dots could be purchased in sheets, and they are cut and applied by the graphic artist to create tonal shading for an area.

18. A: The Deconstructivism architectural movement was a postmodern movement in the 1980s, and it sought to question the preconceived ideas of meanings and symbols. The meanings of things exist in context and change over time, so Deconstructivists sought to challenge these preconceived meanings and challenge the idea of what a building or a structure should look like. Deconstructivist architecture deforms and dislocates what one would normally expect to see.

19. D: Charles-Édouard Jeanneret, who designed architecture under the name Le Corbusier, decided that people should have a functional living space, providing for all their physical and psychological needs. He designed his ideal house, which he described as a "machine for living." It provided sun, space, vegetation, controlled temperature, ventilation, and insulation, as well as protection against noise. His work was eventually dubbed the International Style.

20. C: In this artwork, *St. James Led to Martyrdom* by Andrea Mantegna (c. 1455), a worm's-eye view is being used to provide an unusual perspective on the subjects in the artwork. The people and arch are being viewed from below, rather than at eye level, which gives a different view than usual. Mantegna experimented with different views and perspectives in his work, including extreme foreshortening and bird's-eye view.

21. A: The iconography of an artwork shows what the artwork is about. The images used in an artwork convey what it represents. The meaning, however, depends on how the representation was made (the style of the artwork) and the artist's reason, purpose, or intentions of making these representations. Different works of art can have the same subjects but differ in style and purpose, and they can differ in intentions and meaning.

22. B: Reselling another artist's entire image does not fall under fair use provisions of US copyright law. Fair use may apply in limited circumstances, such as when copyrighted material is used for purposes like education, commentary, criticism, or parody; when only a small portion of a work is used rather than the entire piece; or when a work is repurposed or recontextualized to create new meaning. Several factors are considered when determining fair use, including the purpose of the use, the nature of the work, the amount used, and the effect on the market for the original work. Separately from fair use, images that are in the public domain or designated as openly available for reuse (such as those licensed under Creative Commons) may be used because they are licensed or not protected by copyright—not because they qualify as fair use.

23. B: To make a shade of a color, an artist would add black to that color and make it darker. A tint, on the other hand, would be made by adding white to that color. A variety of shades of blue can be made by adding various amounts of black to blue. A variety of tints of blue can be made by adding various amounts of white to blue. Just by using blue, white, and black, a wide range of tones could be created.

24. D: Macramé is a fabric art technique that involves tying knots in a thread or cord in a geometric pattern. This art form was most popular in the Victorian era, and it is usually done with various types of cord or thicker yarn. Looping material with a hooked needle is crochet. Interlacing long threads on a loom to create a large piece of fabric is weaving, and combining fibers to make a thread or a yarn is spinning.

25. C: The goal of East Asian sumi-e brush painting, or ink wash painting, is to capture the essence or spirit of a subject. The artist is not attempting to reproduce the appearance of the subject or capture the details. Because the painting is done with black ink, the artist is not reproducing the colors either. This technique emphasizes brushwork and the permanence of each stroke while capturing the essence or temperament rather than the representation.

26. A: In early war photography, the subjects of photographs were often moved and staged to create a better and more moving composition. Brady acquired permission to take these photographs on the battlefield from Lincoln himself, as long as Brady financed the project. Brady had assistants throughout his career, and as his eyesight deteriorated, it is thought that many of his later photographs were the work of his assistants, and not of Brady himself.

27. A: Red, yellow, and orange are classified as warm colors, whereas blue, green, and violet are classified as cool colors. Warm colors are associated with daylight, intensity, and happiness, and cool colors are associated with nighttime, cold, and sadness. Warm colors tend to advance in an artwork, but cool colors tend to recede. Artists take these qualities into consideration when using these colors within an artwork.

28. D: Representation is the use of signs that stand for something else in an artwork. Throughout history, artists have represented not what they see as much as what they know or mean. They decide how to represent what they see rather than rendering it faithfully as a camera would. This can be seen in the representation of humans in the artwork of Ancient Egypt, in which people are represented in a culturally agreed-upon way that does not indicate that they were too unskilled to represent them in another way.

29. B: Color is the element that artist Helen Frankenthaler focused most on in her artwork. She worked within the Abstract Expressionism movement, and she was known for her poured paint technique. Frankenthaler poured turpentine-thinned paint onto canvas, creating color wash stains on the canvas. These areas of color were luminous and focused her artwork on the color, not texture, line, or form.

30. C: Many artists' materials are created with pigments that are known to be highly toxic if ingested, inhaled, or even contacted with skin. Manganese violet is manganese ammonium pyrophosphate. Cobalt yellow contains cobalt, which is toxic. Chrome orange contains lead. The cadmium red hue is created to emulate the color of cadmium red, without the toxicity of the cadmium-based pigment.

31. C: The deckle is the removable frame that controls the size of the paper in the papermaking process. This keeps the paper slurry within a certain size on the screen to control the size of the paper that is created. This is also where the term deckle edge comes from, when a sheet of paper has an irregular edge that is created from the manual papermaking process. The edge appears rough and feathered.

32. D: In 1985, the Guerrilla Girls formed as an anonymous art group to fight racism and sexism within the art world. Rather than drawing attention to their identities, they wanted to focus on their cause. They wanted to expose corruption within the art world and begin including more women and people of color within the art community by creating shocking protest art that was seen by a wide audience.

33. A: An icon is a religious painting, usually of one or two subjects, and commonly of saints, angels, Mary, or Jesus Christ. These are common in Eastern Orthodox religions, and they date back to the early days of Christianity. An artwork that is of an arrangement of objects, usually fruit or flowers, would be a still life. A painting of a person, usually just the head and shoulders, is a portrait, and an outdoor scene is a landscape.

34. D: In this scene, the group of five people, which would include the man reclining and the tree, would be considered the foreground. The middle ground of this scene would include the man to the left herding two cows. In the background would be the mountains and other shapes obscured by atmospheric perspective.

35. A: This artwork is an example of foreshortening, which compresses and exaggerates the illusion of depth. This is a method of showing perspective and dramatically shortening the subject, and it is a departure from the frontal view of a subject. Foreshortening showed the distortion that the eye would see from the view at this angle as artists experimented with their subjects in new ways.

36. D: A graphic designer should send a high-quality CMYK file format to a printer, and a .png file will be RGB, not CMYK. The file should be at least 300 dpi, and it should be in the CMYK color mode. A .psd file is the Photoshop file format with the layers still separated and fonts included. A .pdf is also acceptable if the fonts are included and it is saved at a high resolution. A .tif file is also a lossless file format that can be of high enough resolution to print.

37. A: A kylix is a wine drinking cup that is wide and shallow. It may or may not have a slender stem, and the inside was used for painting. A krater is a vessel with a broad body used for watering down wine, and it was often decorated. An amphora is a tall jar with a narrow neck and two handles. A kouros is a type of statue of a young boy, standing, shown facing front and symmetrically posed.

38. C: The Mannerism movement occurred during the late Renaissance, from about 1520 until the end of the 16th century when it was replaced by the Baroque style. Mannerism is characterized by an exaggeration of ideas of beauty and proportion. Figurative artwork is artwork that contains recognizable subjects, such as portraits and landscapes, so this would not apply to the De Stijl, op art, or color field movement artworks.

39. C: The metalworking technique of brazing involves joining two or more metal items by melting and flowing a filler metal with a lower melting point than the adjoining metal. Using high heat to melt two or more adjoining metal items together is welding, and heating them to a high heat and hammering them together is a process called forge welding. Different metal joining techniques are used depending on the metals that are used and the end results that are desired.

40. B: Azulejos are painted, tin-glazed ceramic tiles that are used to decorate and embellish walls, floors, and ceilings in architecture in Spain and Portugal. These were used not only for ornamental purposes, but also for temperature control. These tiles have a Persian influence in their design, with their geometric and floral designs and interlocking patterns. These can be found in churches, homes, restaurants, and palaces.

41. D: A gisant, French for recumbent, is a reclining sculptured form that lies on the lid of a deceased person's tomb. A glory is the general term for the representation of light around a sacred person, and this could be around the whole person or just around their head. Some names for it are aureole, halo, nimbus, and mandorla. These are often depicted in religious artworks, specifically, with saints and holy persons.

42. A: Silver point is a drawing method that involves using a silver-tipped drawing instrument, or a rod of fine silver in a wooden holder, on specially coated paper. This method was first used on manuscripts by medieval scribes. The paper or surface could be coated with rabbit-skin glue, chalk, or lead white. Modern supports could be coated by gesso or gouache. The coating gives the support more tooth and helps give the drawing a darker value than on unprepared paper.

43. D: Restoration describes the return of a building to its original condition, or as close to original as possible. Renovation is the upgrading of a building while restoring its original features, while also including some contemporary needs. Preservation describes the prevention of the destruction or deterioration of a building, and conservation is a term applied to restoring artwork to its original condition, or as closely as possible.

44. B: Paleolithic artists had a few colors available to them, including brown, black, red, yellow, and white. These colors were created from pigments using earth and charcoal mixed with animal fat and saliva. The colors could depend on the mineral content of the rocks and soil nearby. Blue was made in later times out of lapis lazuli, ultramarine, and cobalt, and then later it was made synthetically.

45. C: A pagoda is a multistory tower with multiple eaves, found in South or East Asia. It is usually related to a Buddhist temple. The structure is derived from the stupa of India, which symbolized a sacred mountain. A tall, four-sided stone pillar with a pyramidal top is an obelisk. A small, dome-like structure on top of a building is a cupola. A rectangular terraced temple in ancient Mesopotamia is a ziggurat.

46. C: Although the Classical period of Greek sculpture showed more realistic anatomy, the poses were more stoic, as shown in the *Doryphoros*. The Hellenistic period of Greek sculpture was the pinnacle of naturalism and expressive movement, as shown in many examples including *Laocoön and His Sons.*

47. A: Outsider art is art created by artists who are self-taught and who work outside of the mainstream art world. Historically, some outsider artists have been patients in psychiatric institutions, but many are simply untrained creators working in isolation from the art establishment. Closely related concepts include art brut (or raw art) and some forms of naïve and folk art, though these are not exact synonyms.

48. A: The commodification of art is the creation of artwork into marketable works that can be bought and sold. In the 20th century, art had become a product that involved auction houses, museums, collectors, and galleries. Some art movements began to fight against art becoming a commodity, including performance art, conceptual art, and earth art, which were each time and location specific in their own ways, and they were not able to be bought and sold like paintings and sculptures.

49. D: Thomas Cole, a member of the Hudson River School, painted this landscape titled *Destruction* from *The Course of Empire.* The Hudson River School was a group of American realist artists who painted landscapes from 1820 to 1880. The Cobra Group was a group of Dutch, Danish, and Belgian Expressionists. The Ashcan School were American realist painters who depicted urban life beginning in 1908, and Les Fauves were the artists who created Fauvism.

50. C: Tatting involves using a needle or shuttle to create lace with knots and loops. Tatting can be used to make edging, collars, doilies, and other lace accessories. The technique dates back to the 17th century. Crochet is the technique of making interlocking loops of yarn with a hook. Needlework is any decorative sewing using a needle. Knitting uses needles to create multiple stitches of yarn in a line.

51. D: A pastiche is a work of art created in the style of another artist. It is not a copy of the artist's work, but one with a similar style or motifs. This is different than a fake, as a fake is attempting to deceive a viewer. A decorative motif based on a palm leaf is a palmette. An artwork created in three panels is a triptych. A small model that is created as a trial sketch before creating it as a larger sculpture is called a bozzetto or a maquette.

52. C: The Fluxus art movement during the 1960s and 1970s focused on conceptual performances and an emphasis on the process rather than the end result. The Fluxus movement contributed new media including intermedia, conceptual art, and video art. Some artists included Nam June Paik and Yoko Ono, and participants in the movement included architects, poets, musicians, designers, writers, and more.

53. B: Gesso is a paint that is traditionally white and has pigment, chalk, or gypsum as an ingredient, and it is used to coat a painting surface prior to starting a painting. Gesso can be used to smooth a painting surface because it can be applied in coats and sanded in between coats. It can also be used as a barrier to protect the paint from breaking down the support because oil paints will break down canvas fabric over time.

54. C: An anamorphosis is a drawing that can be viewed with a mirror or lens to change the distorted drawing optically into the normal view. This is often seen as a stretched drawing around a cylindrical vertical mirror, as shown in the example image. The artwork has to be laid out in such a way that when reflected in the mirror, the viewer sees it changed back into the normal view. This can also be accomplished with a sculpture that has to be viewed from a certain angle to see the recognizable image.

55. A: The formalism aesthetic theory is the most straightforward for critiquing modern artwork by analyzing the elements and principles, rather than looking for meaning, emotions, or representation within nonrepresentational artwork. By using the formalism aesthetic theory to critique modern artwork, including color field, minimalist, and other movements, the artwork can be assessed by its success at using the elements and principles.

56. A: One of the criticisms of the Minimalist art movement was that it undervalued art in general by blurring the line between art and everyday objects. Minimalist sculpture was too pared down, according to this criticism, and it was too far removed from what was previously considered as art. Another criticism was that it lacked the qualities that people normally expected to see in artwork, lessening the viewer's experience.

57. D: A spandrel is the triangular area between the outer curve of an arch and the framework. The middle part of an entablature, between the cornice and the architrave, is called the frieze. The ornamental molding commonly found on facades is the cornice. This can also be the molding between a ceiling and a wall. A stylized leaf used as a decorative motif in Renaissance, Greek, and Roman architecture and art is an acanthus.

58. B: Isocephaly is a method of portraying the main figures' heads at the same heights in an artwork or sculptural relief, regardless of their posture or action in the scene. This was popular in Classical Greek artwork, and it comes from a Greek word meaning "like-headed." Gisant is a reclined effigy on a tomb. Chinoiserie is a French term for decoration based on Chinese motifs. Squaring is a technique for transferring a smaller drawing to a larger drawing.

59. B: The Christian art from the Eastern Roman Empire beginning in the 5th century is Byzantine art. This style grew out of classical Roman art, and it was mostly concerned with religious expression. Byzantine art showed religious ideas in sculptural, mosaic, and painting forms. The icons, or small portrayals of religious figures including saints, are the best-known form of Byzantine art.

60. C: This painting, *Virgin of the Rocks* by Leonardo da Vinci, uses pyramidal composition, also called triangular composition, which is a method of grouping the figures so they form the outline of a pyramid. This was a popular compositional technique in Renaissance artwork, especially with

Madonna and Child subject artworks, with the Madonna forming the apex of the pyramid or triangle.

61. A: Glazing is a technique that consists of placing thin layers of transparent paint on top of each other. For this to work, the paint must be transparent, not opaque. Of the white pigments listed, the only pigment that is transparent is zinc white. Titanium white, flake white, and Cremnitz white are all opaque pigments with strong covering power, but they would not be suited for the glazing technique.

62. D: The four basic sculpture techniques are carving, assembling, modeling, and casting. Carving involves chipping or cutting away pieces of a larger material, such as stone or marble. Assembling is an additive technique that involves gathering materials and putting them together to form the sculpture. Modeling is another additive technique, involving building up a soft material, sometimes on an armature. Casting involves melting down a material and pouring it into a mold.

63. C: Scumbling is an oil painting technique of applying a thin layer of an opaque color over an area to produce a softened effect. Applying a glaze over a light area to create a shadow is called sfregazzi. Using a tool, such as a paintbrush handle or palette knife, to scratch through a layer of paint while it is still damp, is called sgraffito. Sfumato is creating gradual transitions between dark and light for a smoky effect.

64. A: An aquarelle is another term for a watercolor painting. Aquatint is an etching process that involves using acid to bite into lines and tonal areas on a metal plate to give the effect of watercolor in the print. An aquamanile is a medieval vessel that is usually made of bronze or brass, and it is in the shape of an animal. An aquagraph is a monoprint technique that uses a water-based medium.

65. B: Realism rejected heightened emotions and exaggerated scenes, preferring to portray accuracy and truth. The realism movement started in the 1850s in France, and it rejected the idea of portraying subjects heroically or sentimentally. Rather, they sought to portray subjects realistically and seriously, bringing attention to all walks of society. Realism rejected the traditions of art and expanded the definition of what was considered art.

66. B: Bauhaus architecture is characterized by, among other things, steel frames, open floor plans, and primary colors. This style was developed in the 1920s and sought unadorned functionality, focusing on function over form. Enclosed courtyards, arches, domes, and arcades are characteristic of Renaissance architecture. Columns, grandeur of scale, and clean lines are seen in Neoclassical architecture. Horseshoe arches, perforated screens, and geometric designs are common in Islamic architectural designs.

67. D: This artwork, *The Shoots of Autumn Crops* by Zinaida Serebriakova, focuses on rhythm with the repeated element of the rows of crops leading to the horizon. Because the repetition is not uniform, this is not considered a pattern. Balance is the visual weight of parts in a composition. Contrast is how parts of a composition differ, and emphasis is how an artist brings attention to a certain part of the composition by making it stand out.

68. A: Kinetic art is art that moves, driven by outside forces including the atmosphere, magnets, motors, or other forces. This category includes Alexander Calder's mobiles, which were suspended and moved by the flow of air around them. He also created kinetic sculptures that would move by cranks and motors. His kinetic art was one of the earliest examples of art that departed from the standard idea of static artwork.

69. A: For a tintype, a direct positive image is made on a thin plate of metal, or tin. For the daguerreotype process, an image is created on a silvered copper plate. To create a calotype, an image is created on paper coated in silver iodide. An ambrotype is an image created on a piece of glass. These are all photographic processes that were used prior to film cameras being invented.

70. C: The greenware stage of clay, also called bone dry, is when clay is in its most fragile state. This is when clay has been shaped and dried, but not fired yet. When clay is partially but not completely dried, it is considered leather hard. When clay has been fired once but it is still porous, it is called bisque. This is when glaze would be added. Clay that is still soft and easily worked is considered plastic.

71. B: Dry mounting involves using a uniform coat of adhesive to affix an artwork, photograph, or print to a backing. Once this is done, it is considered permanent and is not easily removable from the backing. Unless one is using special materials, dry mounting is not considered archival, although it will usually last long enough for most purposes. The materials used for dry mounting can be pricey, and unless someone prefers its specific results, one might prefer to use photo corners or other methods instead.

72. B: If an artist wants to create a loose, sketchy drawing, with sweeping gestures, a soft drawing media would be ideal for this. A Conté crayon, vine charcoal, or soft pastels would all be good choices for this type of drawing because they are all soft media and could be blended easily. A 4H pencil is a hard pencil with a sharp point, which would be better suited for fine-detail work. This hardness of the 4H pencil will make a light mark.

73. B: Sublime in artwork refers to a greatness and magnitude that is difficult for a person to comprehend. Seeing the sublime can make a person feel overwhelmed and feel small in comparison to their surroundings. The sublime brings attention to the beauty of the landscape and the vastness of what surrounds us. It can generate strong feelings inside the viewer, which is what the painters of Romantic landscapes are attempting to evoke.

74. D: Transformation in artwork involves changing an object and presenting it in a new way. Andy Warhol used transformation when he changed everyday objects into artwork by changing the scale, colors, and materials, presenting them as artwork. Juxtaposition is placing an object next to a contrasting object to emphasize it. Using preexisting objects or images with little or no changes is appropriation. Using unusual proportion to call attention to an object is hierarchical proportion.

75. C: Three-point perspective is used to show buildings from above or below. It uses two points along the horizon line, plus a third point above or below depending on how the buildings are being depicted. One-point perspective uses one point along the horizon line. This is often used for roads or railways. Two-point perspective uses two points along the horizon line, and it can have a building directly in front of the viewer.

76. A: For the printmaking process of manière criblée, practiced in the 15th and 16th centuries, the design is punched into a metal plate, creating a white spotted background. A monoprint is made by the artist drawing or painting on a smooth, nonabsorbent surface. For a linocut or woodcut print, material is cut off a sheet of linoleum or wood to create a design. For an etching, lines are cut into a sheet of metal to create the design.

77. A: This sculpture is best described as an open, dynamic form composed of organic shapes. An open form means that this sculpture has inward recesses that the viewer can see through. The dynamic form describes the sense of movement in this sculpture, as opposed to a heavy, static sculpture such as a pyramid or obelisk-type form. The organic shapes are natural, free-flowing shapes, which differ from geometric shapes. This also has interior and exterior contours.

78. B: An armature is the rigid frame that a sculptor might use within a sculpture. This is used for an additive sculpture process, which is when a sculptor adds pieces of material to create a sculpture. This differs from a subtractive method, in which material is removed from a larger piece, such as marble or wood. An armature is used as a foundation around which a malleable material, such as clay, is formed and allowed to dry. The armature is usually made out of metal.

79. C: Composition describes how the artist organizes form in a work of art. This includes where the artist places shapes, areas of light and dark, the subjects, and more. Composition describes how the artist arranges the elements in the artwork and generally how the artwork is arranged and put together. The presentation of shapes in a work of art is the form. Form can also refer to the three-dimensional shape of a sculptural artwork.

80. D: The canting, also spelled tjanting, is a tool used to draw lines in hot wax on fabric for the batik technique. The word batik is Javanese in origin, and it refers to a technique of wax-resist dyeing. Lines are drawn on fabric in hot wax, and then the wax cools and dries. The fabric is dyed, and the wax is scraped or boiled off. This technique is also used in many other cultures. The canting is a small pen-like instrument with a small reservoir and spout for the wax to flow through.

81. B: The creator of this African mask used the principle of design, pattern, to organize the element of art, line. Pattern is a principle of design that describes the uniform repetition of an element of art. If the repetition was not uniform, it could be described as rhythm instead. The principles of design can be used by the artist to organize the elements of art in an artwork. These lines were carved and painted by the artist to be repeated in a uniform way.

82. A: The image sensor on a digital camera is responsible for converting the information of the image detected by the camera into an electronic signal. The aperture changes the size of the lens opening, which changes the amount of light that can reach the image sensor. The memory card in a digital camera stores the image information, and the size of the memory card can vary. The lens is where light enters a camera.

83. C: When oil paints became the new, popular medium, artists began to find new ways to use their old medium, egg tempera. Some used egg tempera as an underpainting for oil paintings. Others combined an egg yolk and oil emulsion called tempera grassa. Others switched back and forth between both media, and oil paints eventually won out due to their slow-drying qualities and ease of use. Unfortunately, many paintings are now mislabeled and only documented as tempera, with no way to tell for sure whether they are egg tempera or what binder was used.

84. A: An advantage of lossy file compression is that the size of the file is reduced, but the file is still recognizable. This makes the file easier to be emailed or published online. If an image needs to be printed, it must be kept as a high-resolution file and will likely be saved as a lossless file format. It would not be pixelated. The file would not decrease in resolution.

85. D: Panel paintings, which consisted of artwork created on either a flat single piece of wood, or pieces of wood joined together, were popular throughout parts of history, including the Middle Ages and the early Renaissance. It fell out of popularity as canvas became a more popular medium. Panels were used to create small icon paintings and larger altarpiece works. They were used for miniatures and small devotional paintings. By the first half of the 16th century, canvas took over as a preferred support for painting in Italy.

86. B: In this example of photo retouching, the man was removed from the photograph for political purposes. Early photo retouching was accomplished not with the help of software, but through manipulation of the negative while creating the print. In this example, the man who disappeared had fallen out of favor and was made to "disappear" by the Soviet press. This photograph shows Stalin, in 1920, to the left in the photograph.

87. B: If a critic describes and analyzes art based solely on its context within the art world, they are using the institutional theory of art. This theory is based on art only having value within the context of the art world or the value that museums and galleries give it. The formalism aesthetic theory is based on how an artwork is analyzed just by the elements and principles. The expressionism aesthetic theory looks at the emotions within an artwork, and the deconstruction theory involves finding hidden meanings and implied messages within an artwork.

88. C: Tessellation is a method of tiling a shape with no gaps or cracks in every direction, potentially infinitely. This is a method used often by M.C. Escher, and it is also seen in Islamic tiles on architecture. The unending tile patterns contain geometry and symbolism, as well as botanical themes, and their ability to be repeated in this way suggests infinity. Tessellation can also be seen in quilting, math, wallpaper, and many other patterns.

89. A: A triadic color scheme consists of three colors spaced evenly on a color wheel, forming a triangle. This is a good choice for beginners because it is easy to balance in an artwork. One color plus the two adjacent to its complement makes a split complementary scheme. Three adjacent colors on the color wheel can make an analogous color scheme. Using colors from within the same color family, either warm or cool, can make a warm or a cool color scheme.

90. D: Depending on the size of the sculpture and the intention of the artist of how it is displayed and viewed, it could be displayed on a pedestal at eye level, on the ground outside or the floor of a museum, or in a glass display case inside a museum or gallery. It is least likely that a stone sculpture would be hung on the wall due to the heaviness of the material and the potential size of the artwork.

91. C: The camera obscura, also known as a pinhole camera, projects an image through a hole in a wall to the other side, but in reverse and inverted. For the image to be clear, the surroundings must be dark. This is sometimes used to safely get a clear image of an eclipse without looking directly at the sun. The camera obscura is a predecessor of the camera, and it came before the daguerreotype and the calotype.

92. B: Sprayed paint poses several hazards to the artist, including the inhalation of the solvent and pigments in the sprayed paint and the flammable propane and propellants contained in aerosol spray paints. Different types of sprayed paints can be used depending on the type of artwork that is being created. An artist can use a water-based paint through an airbrush rather than a can of flammable spray paint. Dust is not an issue with a sprayed paint.

93. C: Paint made from pigment added to heated beeswax is called encaustic. This medium was used by the Egyptians, Romans, and Greeks to paint on walls. Some encaustic mixtures also included linseed oil, damar resin, and other types of waxes. Paint made from pigment mixed with gum arabic as a binder is called watercolor. Paint made by mixing pigment with a drying oil, usually linseed oil, is oil paint. Paint made from adding pigment to an acrylic polymer emulsion is called acrylic paint.

94. A: In this list of sizes presented, 10″ × 20″ is not a standard frame size. Using a standard frame size allows an artist to use standard premade sizes of paper that will fit easily into a premade frame without cutting. These can also be used with precut mats, which will also fit into a premade frame. If artists choose to work with different sizes of paper or stretch their own canvases, they will have to make their own frames or get their work custom framed, which will increase the cost.

95. D: In an intermittent, or periodic, kiln, the kiln is loaded while it is cool, closed and brought up to its desired temperature, and the ware is fired. Then the kiln is cooled, and the door can be opened and the ware unloaded. There are several types of periodic kilns. In a continuous or tunnel kiln, the kiln is kept at a constant temperature while the ware is loaded into cars and slowly brought through the kiln on rails to be fired.

96. B: This would be considered op art, or optical art, which is a style that relies on optical illusions. Op art manages to use lines and colors on flat planes in such a way that it deceives the eye into thinking that the plane is advancing and receding. In this example, the center of the image appears to recede into the distance, although the artist used only black and white in the artwork. Famous artists who used this style include Victor Vasarely, Bridget Riley, and Wen-Ying Tsai.

97. B: The purpose of applying sizing to a canvas is to protect the fabric canvas from the acidic qualities of the paint. Rabbit-skin glue, created with boiled-down animal collagen, was a traditional sizing used for canvas, but there are store-bought alternatives now. After the sizing has been applied, the canvas is primed by applying gesso or another primer, which is traditionally white and provides the surface upon which the artist will paint.

98. A: Stainless steel was invented in 1913. Bronze has been used as a metal for casting, including the lost wax casting method, for centuries. The oldest known example is 6,000 years old. Other metals have been used in various ways for sculptural techniques and for jewelry making since ancient times. Marble has been used for centuries for sculpture, and stoneware is one of the oldest forms of sculpture.

99. D: Form is the presentation of shapes in an artwork, or its shape in three dimensions. In two-dimensional artwork, form has width and height, but in three-dimensional artwork, it also has depth. In two-dimensional artwork, depth in form can be implied through shading and perspective. Shapes can be geometric or organic, and this applies to either two- or three-dimensional artwork. Form should not be confused with size or shape.

100. C: Hierarchical proportion is a type of proportion that shows the hierarchy that the artist intended in the artwork. In this case, the artist is showing the importance of the central figures over the surrounding figures by portraying them proportionally larger. This method was often used in Egyptian artwork, showing the rulers as being larger than those of lower status. It was also used in Renaissance artwork, showing perceived importance as the artist intended.

Practice Test #3

1. The artists Man Ray, Marcel Duchamp, and Max Ernst are all associated with which art movement?

a. Constructivism
b. Dada
c. De Stijl
d. Bauhaus

2. Which of these techniques involves the application of small dots of paint or ink to create patterns or areas of value?

a. Stippling
b. Sgraffito
c. Glazing
d. Impasto

3. Which of the following best describes one of Ai Weiwei's motivations for creating his *Sunflower Seeds* artwork?

a. To expose the benefits of the nutrients of sunflower seeds
b. To create jobs for metalsmiths throughout China who fabricated the seed replicas
c. To provide a large-scale exhibit for an exhibit hall at the Tate Modern
d. To comment on China's mass production techniques that process items for the West

4. Which of the following best describes a change from the Classical period to the Hellenistic period of Greek sculpture?

a. Sculptures were created with a less natural pose.
b. Sculptures showed a more religious purpose.
c. Sculptures showed more emotion, energy, and suffering.
d. Sculptures mainly adorned temples.

5. Which of the following is an accurate statement regarding digital photography versus film photography?

a. Digital photography is slower and more expensive than film photography.
b. Digital photography has more limited storage space than film photography.
c. Digital photography requires specialized equipment for developing the photographs.
d. Digital photography can be more easily edited than film photography.

6. How did a major medical event affect Chuck Close's subsequent painting career?

a. Close modified his techniques to accommodate his restrictions.
b. Close stopped painting and continued to publicize his artwork.
c. Close turned to other forms of artwork instead of large-format painting.
d. Close stopped painting and turned to teaching.

7. Which of the following is an ingredient traditionally used by Renaissance painters to seal a canvas?

a. Tempera
b. Rabbit-skin glue
c. Linseed oil
d. Acrylic

8. Which of the following is NOT a method that is used to create a successful composition in a photograph?

a. The rule of thirds
b. Frame within a frame
c. Boxing it in
d. The rule of odds

9. Which of the following best describes the mezzotint process?

a. The artist uses gouges to cut away the pieces of material that will not hold ink.
b. The artist works from dark to light, roughening and smoothing areas of a plate to change their ability to hold ink.
c. The artist melts fine particles of acid-resistant powdered rosin onto a metal plate, which is then dipped in acid.
d. The artist uses a burin to carve lines into a plate, and these lines hold the ink for printing.

10. Which of the following best describes traditional Japanese raku pottery?

a. High-fired stoneware that is wheel-thrown and fully vitrified
b. Porcelain ware fired at extremely high temperatures to produce a translucent finish
c. Pottery traditionally removed from the kiln while still hot as part of a specialized low-temperature firing process
d. Earthenware that is defined primarily by its red clay body and porous surface

11. Which of the following best describes the artist Jean-Michel Basquiat?

a. He was part of a graffiti duo called SAMO in the 1970s.
b. He created elaborate collages that depicted Harlem.
c. He portrayed slavery in the form of life-sized silhouette artwork.
d. He led a group of artists that began the Minimalist movement.

12. Which of the following is the best description of appropriation in artwork?

a. Placing contrasting elements next to each other
b. Using unusual proportions to emphasize a part of an artwork
c. Borrowing and using pre-existing images with few or no changes
d. Changing an image and presenting it in a new way

13. Which of the following was a tenet of Bauhaus design and architecture?

a. Agility and flexibility
b. Form follows function
c. Structure should appear married to the ground
d. Visual weightlessness

14. Which one of the following pigments is considered toxic?

a. Yellow ochre
b. Burnt umber
c. Chrome yellow
d. Cadmium red hue

15. Which of the following best describes a salon-style exhibition?

a. Artwork is shown in a line at eye level to give each piece equal importance.
b. Artwork is hung slightly above eye level to prevent the line of sight from being obstructed.
c. Artwork is hung at and above eye level to show the artists' reputations.
d. Artwork is hung at, below, and above eye level to maximize the number of artworks shown on a wall.

16. Which of the following is the correct way to write an aspect ratio with a height of 9 and a width of 16?

a. 9:16
b. 9x16
c. 16:9
d. 16x9

17. Which of the following is a term for a preliminary small-scale model created prior to a finished sculpture?

a. Maquette
b. Armature
c. Crucible
d. Majolica

18. Which of the following describes a characteristic that Egyptian and Mayan pyramids have in common?

a. A tiered structure
b. A square base with four sides
c. An exterior of white limestone
d. A temple at the top

19. Which of the following describes an advantage of using gouache instead of acrylic paint?

a. It can be rewet and reworked.
b. It dries to a gloss finish.
c. It dries very slowly and can be worked with for long periods of time.
d. It stays the same color when it dries.

20. What is the difference between PPI and DPI when referring to resolution?

a. PPI refers to parts per inch on a digital screen, whereas DPI refers to dots per inch on a digital screen.
b. PPI refers to pixels per inch on a digital screen, whereas DPI refers to dimensions per inch on a printed material.
c. PPI refers to parts per inch on a digital screen, whereas DPI refers to dimensions per inch on a digital screen.
d. PPI refers to pixels per inch on a digital screen, whereas DPI refers to dots per inch on a printed material.

21. Which photo editing software filter can be used to achieve the effect in this image?

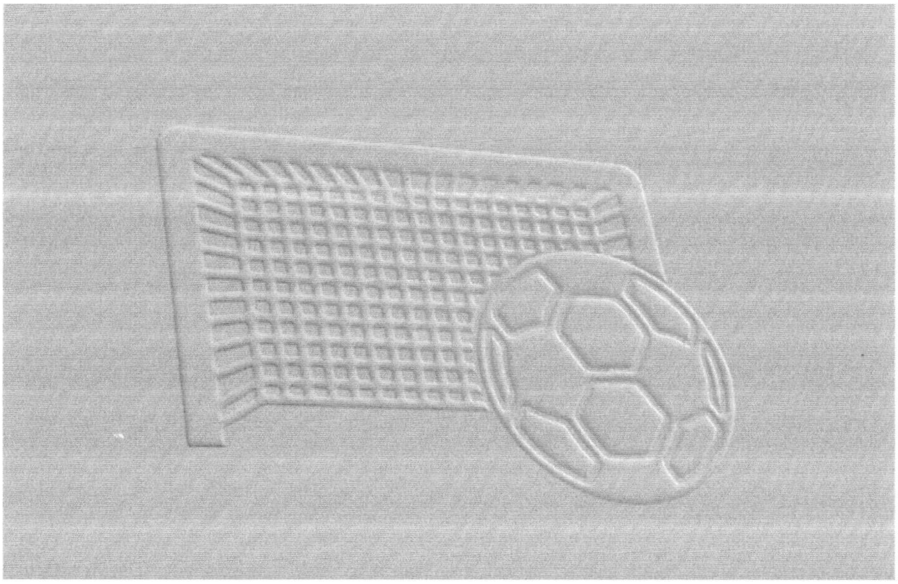

a. Emboss
b. Extrude
c. Glowing edges
d. Trace contour

22. Which of the following does NOT describe warp and weft in weaving?

a. The warp is stretched into place on a loom.
b. The weft is woven through the warp.
c. The weft is longitudinal and is held in high tension.
d. The warp threads must be stronger than the weft threads.

23. An artist is creating a drawing from life. They are keeping their focus entirely on the subject without glancing at the paper. Which type of drawing is this artist creating?

a. Gesture drawing
b. Blind contour drawing
c. Perspective drawing
d. Crosshatch drawing

24. In which art period did the artist's status begin to change from that of a skilled laborer to a more respected and admired profession?

a. Medieval
b. Baroque
c. Rococo
d. Renaissance

25. Which of the following principles of design does this artwork most focus on?

a. Balance
b. Pattern
c. Rhythm
d. Unity

26. How many megabytes are in 1 gigabyte?

a. 1,000 megabytes
b. 10,000 megabytes
c. 100 megabytes
d. 10 megabytes

27. Which of the following is the best use of glassine paper?

a. To create an egg tempera painting
b. To create a detailed pen and ink drawing
c. To place between prints for protection and conservation
d. To cut and glue for collage artwork and assemblages

28. Which of the following theories of art would recognize the subject of this artwork as a girl playing the piano and its importance as an extension of our perception?

a. Expressionism
b. Representationalism
c. Formalism
d. Deconstructivism

29. A color harmony that forms a rectangle on a color wheel, with the four corners on two complementary pairs, forms which of the following color harmonies?

a. Split complementary
b. Tetradic
c. Triadic
d. Analogous

30. Due to an emphasis in African culture on health and strength, many African sculptures portray

a. Youthfulness
b. Geometry
c. Luxury
d. Magnificence

31. Which of the following art movements was the Art Deco movement influenced by?

a. Impressionism
b. Expressionism
c. Cubism
d. Realism

32. Which of the following sculptural methods are considered to be additive processes?

a. Casting, assembling, and carving
b. Carving, modeling, and assembling
c. Casting, modeling, and carving
d. Casting, modeling, and assembling

33. Frida Kahlo was known for using symbolism throughout her many self-portraits. Which of the following themes were common throughout her self-portraits?

a. Pain and suffering
b. Freedom and social change
c. Immigration and migration
d. Industry and progress

34. Which of the following describes the appeal of automatism to surrealist artists?

a. It made drawings much quicker to produce.
b. It brought subconscious thoughts to the surface.
c. It made use of a newly created type of machine.
d. It helped artists use materials in a different way.

35. If an artist wanted to cover a background evenly with watercolor, the best method to use would be:

a. Wet on dry
b. Glazing
c. Wash
d. Dry brush

36. Why are some precious metals often mixed with alloys or plated with rhodium?

a. To improve their appearance
b. To improve their value
c. To make them softer
d. To strengthen the metal

37. Which of the following is an example of post-and-lintel construction?

a. Colosseum
b. Stonehenge
c. Washington Monument
d. Taj Mahal

38. If an artist wanted to create multiple prints using a printmaking technique, which of the following techniques would NOT be appropriate to use?

a. Linocut
b. Screen-printing
c. Intaglio
d. Monotype

39. Which of the following methods was used to create this photograph?

a. Macro
b. Dodge and burn
c. Long exposure
d. Short depth of field

40. Which of the following graphic file formats is an example of lossy compression?

a. .tif
b. .bmp
c. .gif
d. .jpg

41. Which of the following is a reason that canvas needs to be primed prior to being used for oil painting?

a. Without primer, the oil will eventually cause the canvas to deteriorate.
b. Without primer, oil paints cannot be layered as effectively.
c. Oil paints will dry too quickly if the canvas is not primed first.
d. The impasto technique will not work as well without primer.

42. Which of the following color harmonies could consist of green, orange, and purple?

a. Split complementary
b. Triadic
c. Tetradic
d. Analogous

43. Which of the following terms describes a decorative artistic repeating pattern used in Islamic art, which includes rhythmic lines and foliage?

a. Damask
b. Paisley
c. Arabesque
d. Toile

44. An artist wants to capture a ballet performance while it is in progress. Which of the following methods would work best?

a. Oil painting
b. Egg tempera
c. Gesture drawing
d. Pointillism

45. Which of the following architectural styles is characterized by tall spires, stained glass, and flying buttresses?

a. Neoclassical
b. Baroque
c. Italianate
d. Gothic

46. Which of the following is NOT a name for a type of photographic positive created on a thin sheet of metal?

a. Ambrotype
b. Tintype
c. Melainotype
d. Ferrotype

47. Which of the following pigments is NOT hazardous due to the use of toxic metals?

a. Cadmium red
b. Cadmium yellow hue
c. Cobalt blue
d. Flake white

48. Which of the following describes the placing of two visual elements next to each other to create the effect of contrast?

a. Juxtaposition
b. Appropriation
c. Transformation
d. Extrusion

49. If an artist wants to engrave a metal plate for printmaking, which of the following tools would they use?

a. Brayer
b. Intaglio
c. Burin
d. Gouge

50. With which of the following media would this image have been created on a wood panel, in 1546?

a. Acrylic paint
b. Watercolor
c. Oil pastel
d. Egg tempera

51. Which of the following best describes the purpose of a patron for a Renaissance artist?

a. Patrons purchased artwork that had been created by artists.
b. Patrons encouraged artists to explore new media.
c. Patrons commissioned artists to create artworks.
d. Patrons helped artists find sites to create their sculptures.

52. Which of the following binders is used in watercolor paints?

a. Gum arabic
b. Linseed oil
c. Acrylic polymer
d. Turpentine

53. Which of the following is NOT a name for the printing method in which ink is pressed through a fabric with a squeegee onto a substrate below?

a. Silkscreen printing
b. Monoprinting
c. Screen printing
d. Serigraph printing

54. Which of the following stone carving tools would be used for the first "roughing out" step of creating a sculpture?

a. Rasp
b. Hammer and chisel
c. Sandpaper
d. Riffler

55. If a graphic artist wanted to create a logo that could be resized for large banners without becoming pixelated, which of the following would be the best method?

a. Creating a logo in Adobe Photoshop and saving it as a JPEG
b. Drawing a logo by hand and scanning it, saving it as a GIF
c. Creating a vector-based logo and saving it as an EPS
d. Tracing a hand-drawn logo in Adobe Photoshop and saving it as a TIF

56. Which of the following describes the purpose of photography by Farm Security Administration (FSA) photographers during the Dust Bowl?

a. To create artistic photographs for gallery shows
b. To create propaganda photographs of bread lines
c. To document the need for government assistance for the farmers
d. To discourage families from moving to rural areas

57. Which of the following correctly describes the relationship between an element of art and a principle of design?

a. Movement could be created with wavy lines leading the viewer's eye throughout the piece.
b. Shapes could be created with the use of different lines.
c. Texture could be created by the use of different colors.
d. Unity could be created with a similar pattern used through an artwork.

58. Which of the following gave rise to the portrayal of secular figures in Renaissance era artwork?

a. A lack of funding for artists
b. A surge of humanism
c. The death of the Medici family
d. A stronger devotion to the Catholic Church

59. An artwork is analyzed according to how accurately the subject is portrayed. This artwork is being analyzed using which of the following aesthetic theories of art criticism?

a. Emotionalism
b. Formalism
c. Deconstructivism
d. Representationalism

60. Which of the following fibers used in fiber arts is NOT a man-made fiber?

a. Polyester
b. Rayon
c. Acrylic
d. Jute

61. Which of the following is a characteristic that acrylic and oil paints have in common?

a. Acrylic and oil paint can be applied either thickly or thinly to the canvas.
b. Acrylic and oil paint both dry slowly and allow time for the artist to continue to work.
c. Acrylic and oil paint both need turpentine or solvent to clean the brushes.
d. Acrylic and oil paint can both be thinned with water.

62. In this image, especially in the darker areas including the underbelly of the horse and the ground on which it stands, which of the following techniques was used in which the lines intersect as a close set of parallel lines?

a. Stippling
b. Lining
c. Crosshatching
d. Contouring

63. Which of the following is the best reason to float-mount a piece of artwork when preparing artwork for hanging?

a. The artwork goes all the way to the edge of the paper.
b. The artwork is too big to fit into a frame.
c. The artwork is too delicate for framing.
d. The artwork is the wrong size for the frame.

64. In later 20th-century practice, how did the advent of acrylic paints help to facilitate the technique of grattage?

a. Artists were able to repaint over acrylic more quickly after it had dried.
b. Artists were able to scrape and peel acrylic paints from the surface of canvas more easily.
c. Artists were able to mix more water-based media into acrylic paints.
d. Artists were able to mix oil-based media with acrylics to get more interesting effects.

65. Which of the following best describes the balance, emphasis, and movement of the *Red Wire Sculpture*?

a. Symmetrically balanced, with movement following the red wire element clockwise, and emphasis on the red wire
b. Asymmetrically balanced, with movement following the red wire element counterclockwise, and emphasis on the red wire
c. Symmetrically balanced, with movement following the red wire element clockwise, and emphasis on the black sphere at the bottom
d. Asymmetrically balanced, with movement following the red wire element counterclockwise, and emphasis on the black sphere at the bottom

66. Which of the following drawing media was created in response to a shortage of graphite and was created in a range of neutral and sanguine tones?

a. Chalk pastels
b. Charcoal
c. Conté crayons
d. Oil pastels

67. Which of the following types of artwork can be attributed to Aboriginal artists in Australia?

a. Wooden masks, dot paintings, and obelisks
b. Petroglyphs, dot paintings, and stone arrangements
c. Petroglyphs, stone arrangements, and wooden masks
d. Dot paintings, wooden masks, and temples

68. Which type of symmetry is being used in this mandala?

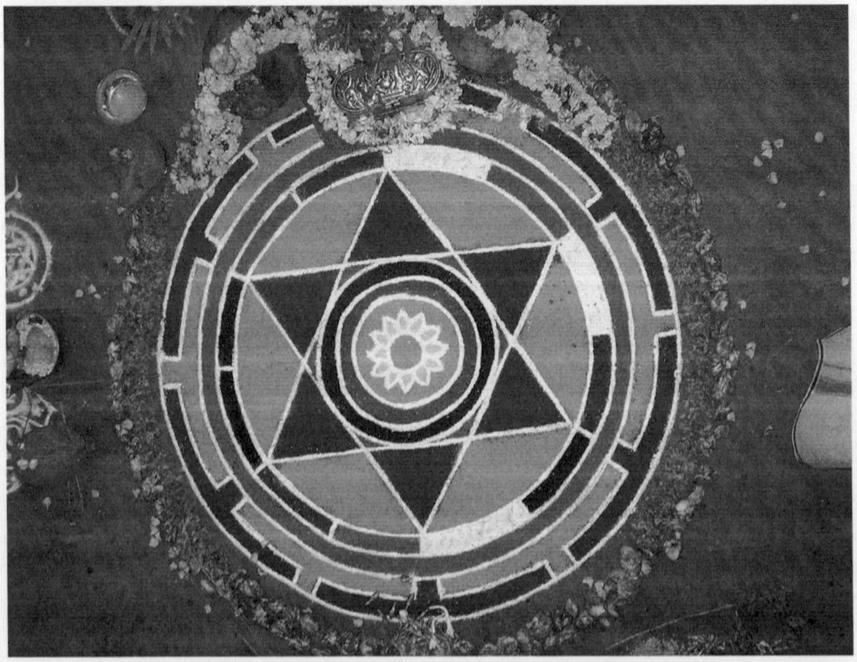

a. Radial
b. Circular
c. Round
d. Diverging

69. Which of the following best describes why hinging tissue or mounting corners are used to hold artwork in place when framing, rather than taping the image on all four sides to the mat?

a. Conservation-grade tape is expensive, and this method uses less tape.
b. Using hinging tissue or mounting corners allows the framer to reposition the image in case of errors.
c. The photo corners can be reused on another image, whereas the tape cannot.
d. When the image, mat, and mat board expand and contract with fluctuations in temperature and moisture, it will not damage the image.

70. Which of the following statements about depth of field in cameras is true?

a. A higher iso setting results in a shallow depth of field.
b. A wide aperture results in a shallow depth of field.
c. A higher shutter speed results in a shallow depth of field.
d. Being closer to the subject results in a large depth of field.

71. Which of the following is NOT a video file format?

a. .avi
b. MP4
c. .wmv
d. .png

72. A student evaluates a well-known artwork, finding the potential hidden meanings and implied messages within it. Which of the following criticism theories is the student using?

a. Formalism aesthetic theory
b. Cultural perspective aesthetic theory
c. Deconstruction criticism theory
d. Expression aesthetic theory

73. Which of the following artists is NOT associated with land art, earthworks, or earth art?

a. Robert Smithson
b. Jackson Pollock
c. Walter De Maria
d. Andy Goldsworthy

74. Which of the following best describes Roy Lichtenstein's motivation for using comic book styling in his artwork?

a. He wanted to close the gap between fine art and commercial art.
b. He was attempting to draw attention to growth in the comic book industry.
c. He hoped to practice creating comic art on a larger scale.
d. He wanted to push the boundaries of copyright by using previously created comic panels.

75. Which of the following scenarios correctly describes the "fat over lean" oil painting principle?

a. Each layer of paint added needs to have less oil and more solvent than the paint underneath.
b. The layers of paint closest to the canvas need to be the most flexible.
c. Each layer of paint added on top needs to be subsequently more flexible than the one underneath.
d. Each layer of paint should have exactly the same oil-to-medium ratio to prevent cracking.

76. Which of the following describes the biggest risk of dealing with clay dust?

a. Clay dust is toxic to the touch, and gloves should be worn.
b. Many types of clay dust can be toxic and can cause respiratory problems if inhaled.
c. Clay dust can irritate the eyes and skin.
d. Clay dust can cause the floors to be slick, so nonslip boots should be worn.

77. Which of the following types of printers will produce the best-quality photo prints?

a. Solid ink
b. Dot matrix
c. Laser
d. Inkjet

78. An art critic analyzes this vase with deliberation over the cultural meanings of the dragon, pine, and bamboo painted on the surface. Which of the following methods is this critic using?

a. Formalism aesthetic theory
b. Cultural perspective aesthetic theory
c. Expressionism aesthetic theory
d. Deconstructivism aesthetic theory

79. If an artist wanted to draw on a lithographic printing plate or stone to create a print, which of the following materials would he or she use?

a. Tusche
b. Gouache
c. Charcoal
d. Conté crayon

80. Which of the following correctly describes the difference between resizing a raster image versus a vector image?

a. Both a raster and a vector image will lose quality if resized.
b. Neither a raster nor a vector image will lose quality if resized.
c. A vector image can be scaled larger indefinitely without loss of quality, whereas a raster image cannot.
d. A raster image can be scaled larger indefinitely without loss of quality, whereas a vector image cannot.

81. Which of the following terms is least associated with crochet?

a. Turning chain
b. Purl
c. Slip stitch
d. Front post

82. This sculpture by Michelangelo from 1513 to 1515 was made out of which of the following materials?

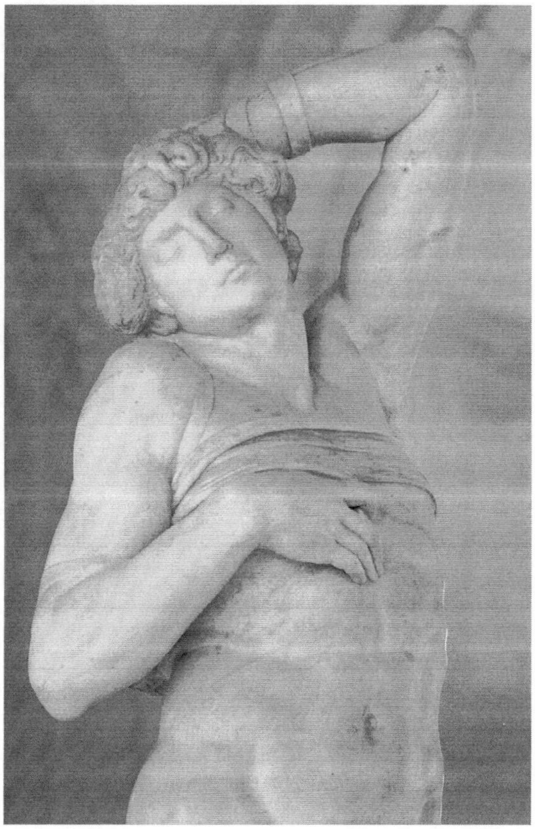

a. Marble
b. Wood
c. Bronze
d. Ivory

83. Which of the following correctly describes the purpose of a baren in printmaking?

a. To cut V-shaped grooves into a block of wood or linoleum before inking for printing.
b. To align the paper onto a plate before running the paper and plate through a press.
c. To etch lines into a plate before rubbing ink into the plate for printing.
d. To transfer the ink onto the paper by rubbing the back of the paper against the ink on the plate.

84. Which of the following types of perspective is being shown in this image?

a. One-point perspective
b. Two-point perspective
c. Three-point perspective
d. Four-point perspective

85. Which of the following describes a strategy for creating a pleasing composition?

a. Divide the image into even rectangles.
b. Use the "eye of the rectangle" method to position the subject.
c. Place the subject in the center of the artwork.
d. Use the background of the image to create a spiral.

86. Which of the following media would an artist use to leave small highlights of white in a watercolor painting?

a. Burin
b. Tempera
c. Liquid frisket
d. Mahlstick

87. Which of the following does SDS stand for when relating to potentially hazardous art supplies?

a. Safety Data Summary
b. Summary of Data Safety
c. Safety Data Sheet
d. Safety Data Synopsis

88. Which of the following is the best example of using appropriation in artwork?

a. Marcel Duchamp's use of a urinal in his artwork *Fountain*
b. Kara Walker's use of silhouettes in *Insurrection!*
c. Yayoi Kusama's use of dots in *Infinity Dots Mirrored Room*
d. David Smith's use of steel in *CUBI VI*

89. Which of the following types of stone is the softest and used often by beginning sculptors?

a. Limestone
b. Soapstone
c. Alabaster
d. Marble

90. Which of the following types of paintbrush bristles would be the LEAST likely to be recommended for watercolor painting?

a. Sable
b. Squirrel
c. Synthetic
d. Hog bristle

91. An artist wants to complete a painting in one sitting, without allowing the paint layers to dry before applying more layers on top. Which of the following techniques would the artist use?

a. Alla prima
b. Trompe l'oeil
c. Sgraffito
d. Sfumato

92. Which of the following best describes the issue that oiling out is used to repair in an oil painting?

a. The oil reacts to a medium used in the painting, causing it to crystallize.
b. The oil runs when the painting is upright, causing the colors to shift.
c. The oil pools in certain parts of the canvas, giving it an oily appearance.
d. The oil soaks into the canvas, leaving the painting looking dull in spots.

93. Which of the following is the correct name for this architectural element of a statue created for use as a column?

a. Balustrade
b. Pilaster
c. Caryatid
d. Obelisk

94. Which of the following best describes the lightfastness of a pigment?

a. The pigment's ability to retain a light value against factors such as heat or water
b. The pigment's color value in relation to other colors
c. The pigment's stability against exposure to light
d. The pigment's resistance to an acidic environment

95. Which of the following best describes the purpose of pyrometric cones in ceramics?

a. To hold ceramic works in place while in the kiln
b. To provide a visual of the level of heat in the kiln
c. To mold ceramic pieces into consistent cone shapes
d. To pierce ceramic works to prevent explosions within the kiln

96. Which of the following fiber art techniques is shown in this image?

a. Knitting
b. Crochet
c. Embroidery
d. Weaving

97. Which of the following materials is NOT comprised of or colored mainly with carbon?

a. Black ink
b. Charcoal
c. Graphite
d. Soft pastels

98. Which of the following terms refers to a quick sketch of a person, which is often used in fashion illustration?

a. Croquis
b. Pochade
c. Plein air
d. Grisaille

99. An artist needs to take a picture and then edit a photo into a variety of formats and sizes for a virtual gallery show. His camera allows him to save the original photo in a variety of formats. Which of the following file formats should the artist NOT store the unedited version in?

a. .tif
b. .jpg
c. .png
d. .bmp

100. Which of the following accurately reflects what DSLR stands for in camera terminology?

a. Default shield lens recorder
b. Diameter size-lens remake
c. Dynamic screen lens render
d. Digital single-lens reflex

Answer Key and Explanations for Test #3

1. B: Duchamp, Ray, and Ernst were all associated with the Dada art movement. Dada artists rejected traditional aesthetics and embraced the irrational and absurd. They sought to challenge traditional artwork and protest war and violence. Duchamp's well-known Dada work is called *Fountain*, and it is a urinal signed "R. Mutt." Man Ray was best known for his photography, and Ernst was an innovator in collage and a pioneer of Dada art.

2. A: Stippling is a technique that involves applying small dots of paint or ink to create a pattern or area of value. Stippling balances the negative space between the dots with the positive space of the dots as the artist places them at varying distances. A higher concentration of dots placed close together can create a darker value, whereas dots placed farther apart can create a lighter value. Stippling can also create a texture in artwork.

3. D: Weiwei had many motivations behind creating his *Sunflower Seeds* artwork, but one of these was to comment on China's mass production that benefits Western countries. *Sunflower Seeds* was made of porcelain, not metal, and it was created by many porcelain artists in China. It also represented the small snacks that even the poorest families were able to share when he was growing up in China.

4. C: The Hellenistic period of Greek sculpture showed a departure from the Classical period and a change in aesthetics as sculptors created an increase in emotion and realism. Figures showed more energy, intensity, and suffering. While religious figures were still important, the Hellenistic period featured sculptures made for a variety of reasons, such as promoting politicians. Rather than decorating mainly temples, sculpture was increasingly used in public places as well.

5. D: Film photography is generally slower and more expensive to work with than digital photography. It requires specialized equipment to produce the prints from film. The storage space is limited to how many exposures are available on the film. Digital photography is easier to edit and manipulate than film photography due to the availability of photo editing software. There are both free and paid programs that can be used to edit photographs.

6. A: In 1988, Chuck Close suffered a spinal artery collapse. He continued his painting career from a wheelchair, and he used modified techniques to continue to create large-format paintings. Rather than his detailed, photorealistic portraits, his new artwork used small abstract elements that visually combined to create a cohesive large portrait. Close overcame his disability and continued his career successfully.

7. B: Rabbit-skin glue was used to coat a canvas to prevent linseed oil from soaking into the fibers and destroying the canvas. This was used in traditional oil painting, and it was created by boiling connective tissue. This was also used as an adhesive. The rabbit-skin glue also helps to tighten the canvas prior to painting on it. Modern painters will usually now use gesso instead of rabbit-skin glue to prepare a canvas.

8. C: Boxing it in is not a compositional technique for photography. The rule of thirds is when a photographer divides an image into three parts both horizontally and vertically, and he or she then places the focal point at one of those places where the lines intersect. A frame within a frame is when the photographer uses an element such as an arch or window to frame the shot and to show depth. The rule of odds is when the photographer uses an odd number of subjects to create a more appealing image.

9. B: For a mezzotint, the artist will roughen and smooth areas of a plate to change their ability to hold ink. The artist works from dark to light, roughening parts for shading and smoothing parts for lighter areas. Using gouges to cut away material describes linocut and woodcut. Melting fine particles of acid-resistant material onto a plate describes aquatint. The use of a burin to carve lines describes the intaglio process.

10. D: Traditional Japanese raku pottery is characterized by a specialized low-temperature firing process in which the pottery is removed from the kiln while still hot. This technique creates the distinctive surface effects for which raku ware is known.

11. A: Jean-Michel Basquiat was an artist who first achieved fame as part of a duo called SAMO, who created graffiti in New York City in the 1970s. They used the tag SAMO and wrote short phrases and poems throughout Manhattan. Basquiat collaborated with Al Diaz, and the cryptic messages slowly became noticed throughout the city. Basquiat and Diaz gained notoriety as the work was discovered, and Basquiat delved into other forms of art, continuing his success.

12. C: Appropriation involves using pre-existing images or objects in an artwork with few or no changes. Marcel Duchamp's "ready-mades" are one example of this. Transformation is changing an object or image and presenting it in a new way. Juxtaposition involves placing contrasting elements next to each other. Hierarchical proportion uses an unusual proportion to draw a viewer's eye to the more important figures in an artwork.

13. B: Walter Gropius and his Bauhaus school are known for the tenet "form follows function," meaning that the shape, or form, of a building should be decided by the purpose it is created for. The phrase is attributed to architect Louis Sullivan, and the idea was later applied not only in architecture but also in product design, furniture design, and software engineering. Bauhaus provided design education that applied to architecture, advertising, typography, and more.

14. C: Chrome yellow is considered toxic because it contains lead, which is a toxic heavy metal. The pigment chrome yellow darkens over time when exposed to air. It is thought that this is why Van Gogh's *Sunflowers* have turned almost an olive green rather than bright yellow. Although cadmium is also toxic, cadmium red hue is a pigment created to mimic the color of cadmium red, without the toxicity.

15. D: In a salon-style exhibition, artwork is hung at, above, and below eye level, sometimes from floor to ceiling, to maximize the number of artworks that can be shown on a wall and to include more artists or artworks. This style was originally established at the Paris Salon in the 1700s. Larger artworks would be hung higher toward the ceiling, and canvases would be tilted slightly toward the floor for better viewing.

16. C: The aspect ratio refers to the proportion of an image or video. An aspect ratio for an image or video is written in a ratio of width to height, or W:H. In this example, the width is 16 and the height is 9, so the correct aspect ratio is 16:9. This is a common aspect ratio for an HDTV display. This ratio means that if the width is divided into 16 parts equally, then the height would be 9 of these parts.

17. A: A maquette is a small-scale rough draft of a sculpture, which is used so the sculptor can work out issues with materials and see the sculpture from different angles prior to creating the full-scale version. An armature is a support used inside a structure, usually made of metal. A crucible is a container that holds molten metal for some casting methods. Majolica is a type of earthenware glazed in opaque white, which is then painted and fired.

18. B: Egyptian and Mayan pyramids have square bases and four sides. Mayan pyramids are tiered and have steps typically leading to a temple at the top, whereas Egyptian pyramids were primarily used as tombs. Egyptian pyramids are smoother and were covered in white limestone with gold at the top. Egyptian pyramids were much larger than Mayan pyramids, and the Mayan pyramids were built much later.

19. A: Gouache, unlike acrylic paint, can be rewet and reworked once it is dry. It dries to a matte finish, which makes it easier to photograph, and it dries quickly, much like acrylics. While acrylic paint typically turns a darker shade as it dries, how gouache paint dries depends on the color, with lighter colors drying darker and darker colors drying lighter. Gouache and acrylic have similarities but also several differences.

20. D: Although PPI and DPI both refer to resolution, PPI refers to pixels per inch on a digital screen, whereas DPI refers to dots per inch on a printed material. A pixel is the smallest element of a digital display, and it is used to measure digital resolution. Dots are created on printed material by printers putting tiny dots of cyan, magenta, yellow, or black on the surface. DPI measures the resolution or density of these dots.

21. A: The emboss filter in the Stylize menu of photo editing software will make the image seem stamped or raised, and it will change the color to gray. The glowing edges filter finds the edges in an image and applies a neon glow to them. The edge brightness, width, and smoothness can be adjusted. Extrude will give a three-dimensional feel to the image. Trace contour finds the edges within the image and traces them with outlines, like in a contour map.

22. C: The warp threads are longitudinal and are held in high tension; thus, the warp threads must be stronger than the weft threads to hold up to this tension. The warp threads are stretched into place in a loom, and the weft thread is woven in and out between these warp threads. The warp threads are vertical (longitudinal), while the weft threads are horizontal. A tool called a shuttle can be used to carry the weft thread through the warp threads for weaving.

23. B: A blind contour drawing involves the artist keeping their focus entirely on the subject in front of them. This allows the artist to strengthen his or her hand-eye coordination and create a contour drawing of the subject while refraining from looking at what is being drawn. This is typically used as a drawing exercise rather than a way to faithfully capture a subject or scene.

24. D: Renaissance artists saw a change in their status from a skilled laborer, much like a carpenter or seamstress, to a more respected and admired profession. Artists in the Renaissance period underwent more formal training than before, first working under an established artist. They were educated and achieved success under the patronage of wealthy families, or patrons, who commissioned their artwork.

25. C: Rhythm is most present throughout this artwork. Rhythm is created through repetition, guiding the viewers eye and incorporating variation. In this artwork, *Rythme, Joie de vivre* by Robert Delaunay (1930), rhythm is created by repeating the concentric circles throughout the painting in different sizes and different colors. For this to be a pattern, the elements would have to be repeated in a more uniform and predictable order.

26. A: There are 1,000 megabytes (MB) in 1 gigabyte (GB). The storage space on a computer or thumb drive might be measured in GB. A kilobyte is 1,000 bytes, and 1 MB is 1,000,000 bytes or 1,000 kilobytes. 1,000 GB equals 1 terabyte (TB), which is a common size for a computer hard drive. These are all standard measures of size for information stored on a computer or other electronic device.

27. C: Glassine is a paper that is used for conservation and preservation. It is thin and glossy, and it is used to interleave between prints or other artwork that is already dry, to protect the artwork from outside elements and each other. It is not very good for drawing or painting due to the slick surface. Glassine is acid free and archival, and it can be found in large sheets that can be used with large works of art.

28. B: The representationalism theory of art claims that artwork needs to represent something that exists to be art. This makes artwork an extension of our perception. The representation does not need to be literal, but the audience should understand the representation. In this painting, Renoir simply and clearly used the subject of a girl playing a piano, which is something the audience will recognize as a representation of something that exists.

29. B: A tetradic color harmony forms a rectangle on the color wheel, with the corners on two complementary pairs. When using this color harmony, it is best to focus on one color and let the others support it. A split complementary harmony uses one color with two on each side of the one opposite on the color wheel. Triadic uses three evenly spaced colors on the color wheel, and analogous uses colors next to each other on the color wheel.

30. A: Because African cultures value fortitude and vitality, they often portray youthfulness in their statues. These values can be traced back to the times when people lived off the land and had to be strong to hunt and survive. Ousmane Sow's contemporary sculptures are a good example of this portrayal of strength, youthfulness, and endurance in the bodies of strong warriors because he builds these structures from a wire frame.

31. C: Art Deco's style was partially derived from the geometry of Cubism, and the colors were influenced by Fauvism. Art Deco also had elements of Constructivism and Futurism. This popular international decorative style spanned the 1920s to the 1940s, and it affected various arts including fashion, architecture, furniture, and graphics. The structure of architecture was based on geometric shapes and incorporated new materials including aluminum, stainless steel, and lacquer.

32. D: Casting, modeling, and assembling are considered to be additive sculptural processes, whereas carving is a subtractive process. Additive processes consist of adding materials to the sculpture to create the final product, whereas subtractive processes consist of subtracting materials. When carving, the sculptor carves or chips away stone or wood to remove pieces of material and arrive at the desired product.

33. A: Frida Kahlo expressed pain and suffering throughout her art career in symbolism in her paintings. She was in an accident when she was young, and she had lifelong medical issues. She had a volatile relationship with artist Diego Rivera and was unable to have children. Many of her paintings dealt with the pain and suffering relating to her medical issues and her relationship with Rivera, as well as her miscarriages.

34. B: Automatism helped artists tap into the subconscious, which appealed to surrealist artists. In theory, artists would let their subconscious dictate the artwork by creating spontaneous artwork directly from the mind. In reality, the artist would still use some degree of intervention to create work that was aesthetically pleasing. This artwork was not representational and was thought to represent underlying dreams and the psyche.

35. C: A wash involves painting a large area in one or two colors, usually for a background or sky area. This can be achieved by using a broad, flat brush and laying wide strokes of color. If using two colors, this can be done as a gradient. A wash can also be done with ink or acrylics, and it will involve using watered-down paint or ink and painting flat areas of this watered-down pigment or ink.

36. D: In jewelry making, precious metals are often mixed with alloys or coated with rhodium (such as with white gold) to strengthen the metal and make it more durable. Gold and silver on their own are soft and malleable, so they are mixed with metals such as nickel, copper, and zinc to improve their strength and durability and improve their ability to hold gemstones. This also makes them easier to work with.

37. B: Stonehenge is an example of post-and-lintel construction. Post-and-lintel is a building system in which a horizontal element is supported by vertical elements. This is also seen in Ancient Greek architecture and in other examples throughout history. Stonehenge is an example of Neolithic architecture from roughly 3000 to 2000 BC. The later development of the arch allowed for larger structures to be supported.

38. D: The monotype method of printing is not used to make multiple prints. To create a monotype print, the artist draws or paints on a smooth, nonabsorbent surface, then the media is transferred to a sheet of paper. This is done by hand or with a printing press. Linocut, intaglio, and screen-printing are all printmaking methods used to make multiple prints.

39. C: Long exposure is a useful technique for night photography. When using this technique, it is best to use a tripod and a wide-angle lens. The aperture should be set small to keep the elements sharp. The photographer can experiment with the times of exposure to capture light trails of stars, traffic lights, and other lights. The resulting effect will show a sharp image of the still elements and longer trails of lights.

40. D: A .jpg file is an example of lossy compression in a graphic file. Lossy compression will result in a significantly reduced file size, but once information is lost from a graphic file, it cannot be retrieved. Lossless compression refers to when files are compressed without losing any quality. Examples of this type of compression include .tif, .gif, .bmp, and .raw. This will result in larger files than lossy compression.

41. A: Without the primer as a buffer between the oil paint and the canvas, the oil will soak into the canvas and eventually eat away at the fibers of the canvas. Acrylic paints, on the other hand, will benefit from a smoother surface that is created by primer, but they do not necessarily need primer in the same way that oils do and will not affect canvas in the same way. Gesso or rabbit-skin glue is often used as a primer on canvas.

42. B: A triadic color harmony consists of three colors spaced evenly apart on the color wheel. One example of this could be green, orange, and purple. This could also consist of the primary colors, blue, red, and yellow. A triadic color harmony is best used by allowing one color to dominate and using the other two colors to support or accent the dominating color.

43. C: An arabesque pattern is used often in Islamic art, and it consists of a floral pattern, often with lines and leaves that can be repeated seamlessly. The pattern can be extended infinitely, which starkly contrasts with man's finite existence on earth. Islamic art uses these patterns because depicting human and animal forms is discouraged. The word arabesque derives from an Italian word meaning Arabic style.

44. C: Gesture drawing would work best to quickly capture the action of a ballet performance. Oil painting, egg tempera, and Pointillism would all take more time and attention to materials than gesture drawing would. Gesture drawing is meant to capture a figure in motion. The artist can use sweeping motions of the arm to capture the action and direction of the figure and to make quick studies of figures. These can later be used for more detailed artwork.

45. D: Gothic architecture was a style used in Europe during the 12th to 16th centuries. It was characterized by stained glass windows, vaulted ceilings, flying buttresses, and spires reaching toward the heavens. Gothic architecture was heavily used for churches and cathedrals, and it was used to create some of the most distinctive buildings throughout Europe. This style abandoned the thick walls of Romanesque architecture.

46. A: An ambrotype is a photographic process created on a piece of glass. This process was introduced in the 1850s, and it was followed in the 1860s by the tintype, which is also called a melainotype or ferrotype. A tintype is a direct photographic positive created on a thin sheet of metal, coated with collodion-nitrocellulose. Tintypes were popular in the 1860s and 1870s and are still used as a fine-art medium today.

47. B: When a paint is labeled as 'hue,' it is created to look as visually similar to its hazardous counterpart as possible but created without the toxic metals. Cadmium orange hue will be similar to cadmium orange in color but will not contain a hazardous metal. Flake white contains lead which is a hazardous metal. Cadmium and cobalt are also toxic metals and should be handled with care.

48. A: Juxtaposition describes a method of placing two visual elements next to each other to create a contrasting effect. This can help draw attention to the elements, or it can help one stand out more. Juxtaposing two complementary colors can make the colors stand out and can create a jarring effect. Juxtaposing light and dark values, different textures, and other visually opposing elements can draw the viewer's eye and help the artist create a focal point.

49. C: A burin is an engraving tool used to create lines in a metal plate for printmaking. This type of chisel will often have a mushroom-shaped handle to grip and a steel shaft with a sharp cutting point. It can be used to create a V-shaped groove in a copper plate. Burrs are left behind with the lines, which are then removed with scrapers and burnishers to make a smoother surface.

50. D: This image was created with egg tempera in 1546, and it was painted on wood panel so that the egg tempera would be less likely to crack over time. This was the main painting medium for panels up until the 1500s when oil painting became more popular and began to replace tempera paint. Egg tempera uses the yolk and pigment, and it must be prepared right before using.

51. C: During the Renaissance, patrons would commission artists to create artwork and tell the artists exactly what they wanted created. The wealthy Medici family were responsible for a majority of arts patronage in Florence during this time, supporting artists including Michelangelo, Donatello, and Raphael. They were one of the richest families in Europe, and their patronage allowed artists to work without being concerned about money.

52. A: Gum arabic is the binder that is used to hold watercolor paint together with the pigment. It is also often used in gouache paint and soft pastels. These would all be paints and artists' media that could be water soluble and reworked with water. Linseed oil is more commonly used as an oil painting medium, and acrylic polymers are used in acrylic paints. Oil and acrylic media cannot be rewet or reworked.

53. B: Screen printing is also called serigraph printing, serigraphy, or silkscreen printing. This is a method in which the artist presses ink through a fine mesh screen with a squeegee onto a substrate below, and this can be done onto many surfaces including fabric, walls, and electronics.

Monoprinting involves creating a single print, unlike other printmaking methods which can make multiple copies of prints.

54. B: A sculptor will begin "roughing out" their sculpture with some sort of hammer and chisel, which could include a point chisel or a pitching tool combined with a driving hammer. These will be used to break off larger chunks of stone and begin to shape the sculpture. As the sculpture takes shape, the sculptor will take off smaller pieces and refine it, then finally polish it with sandpaper to finish the sculpture.

55. C: To create a scalable logo that will not become pixelated at any size, it is important to create a vector-based logo. This can be done in Adobe Illustrator or other programs. An image in vector format can be rescaled to very large or very small without any loss of quality, unlike a raster image that is made up of pixels. A raster image can generally only be scaled down without loss of quality.

56. C: The Farm Security Administration sought to capture the raw emotion of how the Great Depression and the Dust Bowl were affecting the farmers on the Great Plains. This also helped to document the need for government assistance and show the realities of farm life to the city dwellers. While the photographers helped to justify the government assistance, they also showed the strength and determination of those living through the tough times on those farms and rural areas.

57. A: This example is the only one that uses an element of art and a principle of design. In this example, movement is a principle of design, and lines are an element of art. Lines can be used to create movement in the artwork. Shape, texture, and color are elements of art, whereas unity and pattern are principles of design. The principles of design are used to organize the elements of art in an artwork.

58. B: Secular figures were portrayed more in Renaissance art as the artists moved away from sacred figures and humanism was on the rise. This caused a shift away from a focus on the church and more toward classical antiquity and other subjects. Artists began portraying other subjects rather than focusing only on sacred church-based artwork. Humanism focused more on education and the freedom to create.

59. D: The representationalism aesthetic theory recognizes the importance of the viewer understanding and recognizing the subject of an artwork. For example, if an artist wishes to show the subject of a landscape or a person sitting in a chair, he or she will clearly express this subject, and the viewer will be able to clearly receive this message from the artist. The artist will be able to represent the message to the viewer.

60. D: Jute is not a man-made fiber. It is considered a bast fiber, which is a plant fiber collected from the inner bark or skin of a plant. Other examples of bast fibers include hemp, nettle, and ramie. Jute is used to make burlap or gunny cloth; it is a long vegetable fiber that can be spun into strong, coarse threads. The fibers are tan to brown, and it is generally affordable.

61. A: Acrylic and oil paints can be applied thinly, as a glaze, or thickly, in an impasto style. Oil paint will dry very slowly and allow more time for the artist to work with the painting, whereas acrylic will dry more quickly, usually within 24 hours. Oil paints require turpentine or another solvent for cleaning, whereas acrylics can be thinned and cleaned up with water. Oil paint can be thinned with oils including linseed oil if the artist wants to achieve other effects.

62. C: Crosshatching involves creating sets of parallel lines that cross each other at perpendicular angles. Because these lines are created as closer sets, the illusion of a darker value is created. Lines created farther apart can create a lighter value. The artist can control the value throughout their piece by using hatching and crosshatching throughout a drawing or etching and by varying their techniques as well.

63. A: When float-mounting an artwork, the edges of the artwork are not covered by the frame. The artwork is fixed to a piece of matboard, and then the matboard is put into the frame with the edges of the artwork still showing. This is done when the artwork goes all the way to the edge of the paper and the artist does not want to obscure these edges by the frame, which will always hide a little on each edge.

64. B: Grattage is a Surrealist technique used by Max Ernst and Joan Miro. It involves scraping or lifting paint to reveal textures underneath. Although it was originally developed using oil paint, later artists found that acrylics made the technique easier to execute because acrylics dry into a flexible surface that can be scraped or peeled more effectively. The resulting textures were then used as a basis for further creative development in the composition.

65. D: In this example sculpture titled *Red Wire Sculpture*, the balance is asymmetrical because it is not the same or a mirror image on both sides. The movement is following the red wire counterclockwise as it tapers off on the left side and points down to the focal point. The emphasis of this sculpture, where the movement leads and which draws the viewer's eye, is on the black sphere at the bottom.

66. C: Conté crayons were created in 1795 by Nicolas-Jacques Conté because of a shortage of graphite. They were comprised of a combination of graphite and clay and were made in a range of neutral colors and sanguine tones. They have been used for sketches, studies, and finished drawings, and they can be used on a middle-value paper, with a white Conté crayon providing the lighter values in the drawing. They are frequently used on rough paper and with a painterly style.

67. B: Aboriginal artists in ancient Australia were known for creating petroglyphs, dot paintings, and stone arrangements, among other types of artwork. They were not known for creating wooden masks, obelisks, or temples. Aboriginal or indigenous artists in Australia also created rock paintings, weavings, ceremonial clothing, sand painting, and string art. They often depicted animals and humans in their rock engravings and paintings. Dot paintings are also called papunya art and can depict patterns or representational subjects. They also relied on symbols to relay meaning. Many of these traditions and practices are still prominent in Aboriginal art in Australia today.

68. A: Radial symmetry is a type of symmetry in which elements are arranged to radiate from the center of the artwork. This falls under the principle of balance and is a type of symmetrical balance. A starfish and a bicycle wheel each have radial symmetry. Mandalas are a common type of artwork that contain radial symmetry. Mandala is a word in Sanskrit that means "circle," and mandalas are often composed of many geometric forms.

69. D: With fluctuations in temperature and humidity, the mat, mounting board, and image will all expand and contract at different rates. If the image is attached securely to the board by means of tape, it can damage the artwork as the different materials expand and contract. If hinging paper tissue or photo corners are used, the image will be safe and will not be damaged by these temperature and humidity fluctuations.

70. B: A camera's aperture, or f-stop setting, is the primary means to determine the depth of field in a photograph. The depth of field shows the range over which the objects appear in focus from the foreground to the background. A wide aperture, which is a lower f-stop value, will create a shallow depth of field in a photograph, whereas a narrow aperture, which is a higher f-stop value, will create a large depth of field, meaning more of the picture will be in focus. The camera's aperture changes the size of the lens opening, which controls the amount of light that passes through the lens and reaches the image sensor. A secondary means of changing depth of field is by moving toward or away from the subject. Moving toward a subject results in a shallower depth of field, and moving away from a subject will increase the depth of field.

71. D: Of the listed formats, .png (Portable Network Graphics) is not a video format. The .avi extension stands for Audio Video Interleave. It is an old format that contains audio and video for playback together. The MP4 extension is of high quality and uses lossy compression to provide high-quality video with relatively small file size, and it is a popular format for sharing videos across many platforms. The .wmv extension uses Windows Media Video compression, which is less commonly used.

72. C: The deconstruction criticism theory involves finding hidden meanings and implied messages within an artwork. This theory seeks to analyze what is hidden, omitted, or repressed within the artwork and shows that the initial impression of the artwork is just one of many potential interpretations. The artist's intentions, and the significance of subjects, objects or locations, could all lead to different interpretations of the artwork.

73. B: Robert Smithson, Walter De Maria, and Andy Goldsworthy are all prominent artists in the land art, earthworks, or earth art movements. These movements focus on combining artwork with the landscape and using natural materials from the surrounding area to create the artwork. Other outside materials can also be introduced, although this is not necessary. These works might bring environmental issues to the attention of the viewer, and they are often time sensitive, meaning that time and weather will wear the artwork away. The best-known artist of this genre, Robert Smithson, is known for his work *Spiral Jetty*.

74. A: Roy Lichtenstein spearheaded the Pop Art movement and began to close the gap between commercial art and fine art. He worked as a draftsman prior to his career in art. Lichtenstein used this comic style on a large scale, including the bold lines and colors and the Ben-Day dots, to create a new kind of artwork that was highly criticized for its simplicity and coldness. At the same time, his style is recognized as helping to usher in a new style of artwork.

75. C: The fat over lean principle in oil painting states that layers of paint with the most fat, or oil, should be on top of the leanest layers. Lean layers contain less oil and are often thinned with solvent so they dry faster. In each subsequent layer, the amount of oil medium (fat) is increased, causing each new layer to dry more slowly and remain more flexible. If a fast drying, lean layer is placed over a slower-drying, fat layer, the top layer can crack as the underlying layer continues to cure.

76. B: Although clay dust can be a hazard on the floor and can irritate the eyes and skin, the main issue is that many types of clay dust can be toxic and can cause respiratory problems if inhaled. Silica powder can cause silicosis over time. Inhalation of kaolin powder can cause kaolinosis. Some other materials can contain asbestos, which is also dangerous to inhale. A proper respirator should be used at all times when dealing with clay dust, and the filter cartridges should be changed regularly.

77. D: Although laser printers have come a long way, inkjet printers are still known for producing the best-quality photo images on glossy photo paper. The ink cartridges can be expensive, and the paper trays do not hold a lot of paper. They are also much slower than laser printers. Laser printers are great for printing sharp text in black and white and can print quickly at high volumes. They cannot use a wide variety of paper like inkjet printers can, though.

78. B: The critic is using the cultural perspective aesthetic theory to analyze the symbols painted on this vase. The dragon, bamboo, pine and other symbols hold cultural significance to the Chinese people. The dragon can represent fortune and luck, while pine is a symbol of longevity. Bamboo represents virtue. This theory is concerned with the cultural norms associated with the artist and how they express them in their work.

79. A: Tusche is a medium created by mixing ink with grease for creating lithographic prints. It can be made into the form of a stick for drawing or into a liquid form. Lithography is a form of printing in which parts of the surface are treated to repel the ink. The process is based on the fact that water and oil do not mix. Offset lithography involves an intermediate sheet so that the image is reversed twice before it is printed onto a surface.

80. C: A raster image is made of pixels, and scaling it larger will cause it to look pixelated or blurry. More pixels cannot be created to fill it in and make it look clearer. Photographs will be raster images. A vector image, on the other hand, is made up of points and lines that keep track of their positions in relation to each other. These are infinitely scalable up or down without any loss of quality. Fonts and logos will usually be vector graphics.

81. B: Purl is most commonly a knitting term, and it is one of the types of knitting stitches made with knitting needles. A turning chain in crochet is a chain stitch used at the beginning of the row to bring the yarn to the correct height to work the rest of the row. A slip stitch is a short stitch used as a technique usually to join two pieces or the end of one part to another. The term front post is used for when stitches are worked into the front of a double or triple crochet stitch instead of into the top.

82. A: Although Michelangelo did occasionally work in other materials, the overwhelming majority of his works were carved from marble, including his most famous works of *David, Pieta, Moses, Bacchus,* and this example, *Dying Slave.* Michelangelo's father owned a marble quarry, and it was here that he began to enjoy working with the medium. He became a master of the medium and created many exquisite, lifelike figures out of this cold, hard substance.

83. D: To use a baren for printmaking, first the plate is inked and a piece of paper is placed on top of the plate. Then the baren is rubbed onto the back of the paper to transfer the ink onto the paper. The baren is usually disc-shaped and flat with a handle. If a baren is not available, a wooden spoon can be used or the bottom of a flat, smooth jar or mug. The print could also be run through a press instead of being printed by hand.

84. A: One-point perspective is when there is only one vanishing point at the horizon line and all lines can be drawn back to this point. In this image, the vanishing point would be in the center of the opposite end of the tunnel. All of the lines of the bricks, columns, and tunnel could be drawn back to that one point. This is often the first type of perspective that is learned to show the illusion of depth for roads and train tracks.

85. B: One way to position a subject in a pleasing way is to use the eye of the rectangle method. Draw both diagonals of the rectangle, which divide it into four equal triangles. Each diagonal is split into two line segments at their intersection; mark the midpoint of each of these four segments. These four points are the 'eyes' of the rectangle, where placing a subject often creates a pleasing composition. Many artists have positioned their subjects in this way to create visual interest.

Subjects are not usually positioned in the center of an artwork, and artworks are not usually divided into even rectangles unless one is creating a triptych.

86. C: Liquid frisket can be used to leave highlights on a watercolor painting without having to carefully paint around these small highlights. The artist can first paint the liquid frisket onto the white paper and let it dry. He or she can then paint the watercolor painting over the frisket and allow the watercolor to dry as well. The frisket is like a layer of dried rubber, and it can be rubbed off of the paper, revealing the white paper underneath which has been masked off from and protected from the paint.

87. C: SDS stands for Safety Data Sheet (formerly Material Safety Data Sheet [MSDS]), and they contain information on the potentially harmful effects of exposure to materials as well as the proper safety procedures for handling these materials. Not all materials require this information, but when this information is provided in the form of an SDS, it is important to read and understand it so that the risks and procedures for using the materials are fully understood.

88. A: Appropriation involves taking an object or an existing artwork and using it in an artwork after changing the original object very little, if at all. When Marcel Duchamp created *Fountain,* he took an already created urinal and signed "R. Mutt" on the bottom, then he called it his artwork. This is an example of appropriation, and it is also an example of rejecting the traditional ideas of what art is and should be. Duchamp called this concept a readymade.

89. B: Soapstone has a hardness of 1-2 on the Mohs scale, and it is often used for beginning sculpting. This type of stone is easily worked, but it is not as durable as other stones.

Limestone has a hardness of 3-4 on the Mohs scale, and along with sandstone, it is categorized as a sedimentary stone. These are both used for sculptures. Alabaster has a hardness of 1.5-2 on the Mohs scale, and it can be translucent when carved. Marble is harder, at a 3-5 on the Mohs scale. Marble has been used frequently since the time of the Classical Period of Greek sculptors.

90. D: Hog bristle brushes are coarse and stiff and are best suited for painting with oils and acrylics. Watercolor paints are usually used with softer bristles, such as those from sable, squirrel, ox, or goat. Kolinsky sable is the most expensive, and it actually comes from the Siberian weasel. It has the ability to hold a fine point, which is a sought-after characteristic for round watercolor brushes. Synthetic brushes come in a wide range of sizes and prices and can be a good choice for any type of paint.

91. A: Alla prima, which is Italian for "at first," is also known as a wet-on-wet technique or direct painting. This technique is used to complete a painting in a short time, and it lends a freshness and spontaneity to the artwork. This could be useful for a portrait study, so the subject does not have to pose for long periods of time. The technique was pioneered by Frans Hals in the early 1600s. Prior to his new technique, visible brushstrokes were rarely seen in paintings.

92. D: Oiling out involves fixing the issue of the oil soaking into the canvas and giving the painting a dull appearance. This is also known as sinking, when the oil sinks to layers underneath. This can be caused by a surface that is too absorbent, using too much solvent, or not using enough medium in the painting. To use this oiling out technique, the artist can paint a thin coat of medium over the painting to restore the sheen and colors.

93. C: A caryatid is a sculpture of a draped female that is created as a column. This architectural element was first used in Greek architecture. A balustrade is a series of pillars that support a rail, sometimes on a balcony. A pilaster is a flat, upright element that appears as a column attached to a wall. An obelisk is a tall, freestanding four-sided structure that ends in a pyramidal point.

94. C: Lightfastness is a pigment's chemical permanence against long exposure to light. This is not the same as a pigment's permanence, which is its ability to hold up to other environmental factors such as water, heat, acid, or mold. Different pigments will have different lightfastness ratings, which can be taken into account by the artist and can affect the artist's choice of media. This also affects how the artwork should be displayed and exposed to outside elements.

95. B: Pyrometric cones are devices used when firing ceramic works within a kiln. They are used to visually gauge the heat within the kiln. These cones have a triangular base and are often used in pairs or groups of three depending on the intent of the artist. The cones are made of materials that will bend when they reach a certain temperature, indicating that the kiln has reached that temperature for firing the ceramics.

96. A: This image shows the knitting technique. Knitting involves using knitting needles, usually two, but this can vary depending on the technique. Knitting creates loops of yarn in a tube or a line, and it is often used for textile work. Each new row creates new loops through the prior row of loops. A wide variety of yarn can be used, as well as several different techniques and stitch types. The basic stitches in knitting are called knit and purl.

97. D: Black ink is carbon black suspended in water or a media, and graphite and charcoal are both composed of carbon. Carbon is a nonmetallic chemical element that has been used in many art materials. Soft pastels, however, are made of many different materials including a powdered pigment and a binder. One binder often used is gum arabic, which is also used in watercolors. Gypsum or chalk is also often found in soft pastels.

98. A: Croquis is a term for a quick sketch of a live model. This is a French word that means "sketch." In fashion design, croquis follow specific proportions, usually making the figure nine heads tall to make them appear tall and elongated. Pochade is a term for a quick landscape sketch to capture the fleeting effects of light on the land, and this sketch can be used for a more finished piece later. Plein air refers to painting outdoors, and grisaille is a monochromatic oil painting often used as an underpainting.

99. B: Of the file formats listed, .jpg is a lossy format, meaning that when it is saved and compressed, information in the image is lost. These files are well suited for keeping files small and easy to manage and can look good on the web, but once the information is gone, it cannot be retrieved. That means that it is good for a final image to be displayed, but .jpgs are not very good for large-scale editing. The compression can cause inaccurate colors and distortions to appear in the final image. The other formats, .tif, .png, and .bmp, are lossless, meaning that they will not lose information when saved. When submitting artwork to be judged, it is best to send the clearest image possible.

100. D: In camera terminology, DSLR stands for digital single-lens reflex. A DSLR camera combines the single-lens reflex camera mechanisms with a digital image sensor. The camera is able to capture images directly as a digital format, rather than onto film. DSLR cameras allow the photographer to see their photographs instantly, and the camera memory is able to hold more images than film cameras could.

Color Images and Additional Materials

Want to take this practice test in an online interactive format?
Check out the online resources page, which includes interactive practice questions and much more: **mometrix.com/resources719/artpq**